**ALTERNATIVE
MOVIE POSTERS II**
MORE FILM ART FROM THE UNDERGROUND

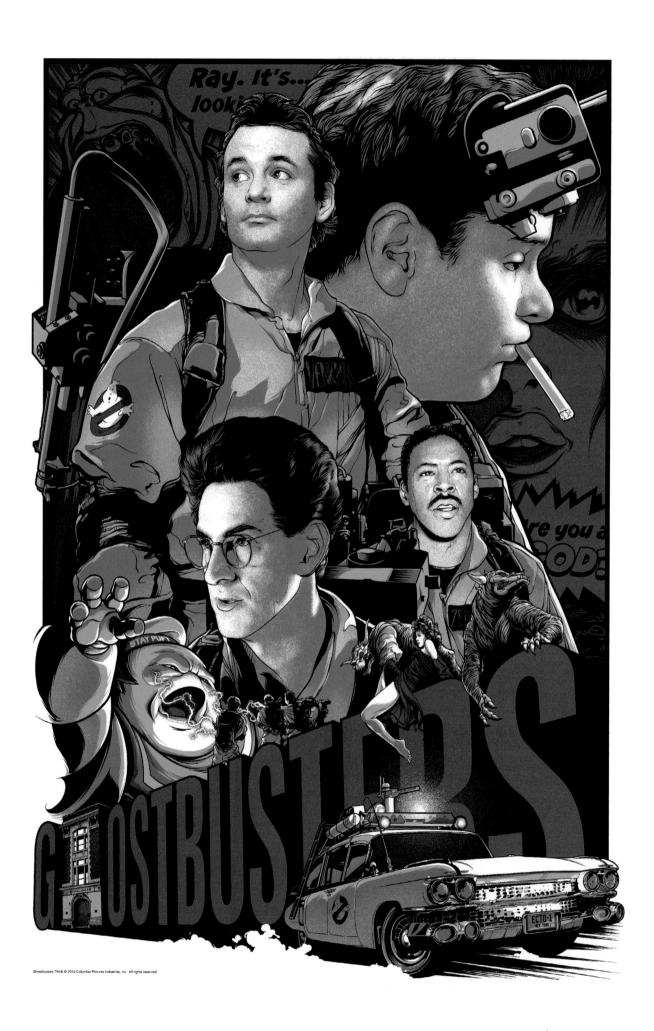

ALTERNATIVE MOVIE POSTERS II
MORE FILM ART FROM THE UNDERGROUND

MATTHEW CHOJNACKI

Ghostbusters / Joshua Budich (pp. 192–193)
24 × 36 in (61 × 91 cm)

Schiffer Publishing Ltd

4880 Lower Valley Road • Atglen, PA 19310

The saga continues...

A few weeks after the first volume of *Alternative Movie Posters* was released, I had already hoped to release a sequel. It had been such a fantastic ride curating and editing the book, meeting the artists, and promoting the alternative movie poster movement in any way possible. Thanks to you guys, you are currently holding volume two.

I was humbled by the amount of press coverage for volume one, not only in the Americas and the UK, but also in the Philippines, Spain, Australia, Indonesia, Africa, and elsewhere. Some of the posters were loved, while others were just "liked," but all agreed on one sentiment: the mainstream movie poster is indeed a lost art form. Legendary poster artists such as Drew Struzan and Saul Bass are sorely missed, but in their absence have very obviously influenced an eager generation of outstanding film artists.

Those close to the industry also picked up the book, whether for inspiration, new art contacts, or simply to secretly admire what could be. In fact, nearly fifty percent of volume one book buyers were in Los Angeles, which I both appreciated and was surprised by.

The book became a guide for the players in the film art scene, and this particular group of artists (and their legions of fans) couldn't be more genuine. It was refreshing to see. I had never witnessed such an enthusiastic network of artists working together so closely—whether to film a documentary (Kevin Burke's *Twenty-Four by Thirty-Six*), to contribute posters for group gallery shows, or to share vendor tables at comic cons and horror conventions. There's even a film art collective, the Poster Posse (PosterPosse. com), working as a unit to bring awareness to the art form; featured artists include Chris Garofalo, Matt Ferguson, Paul Ainsworth, Orlando Arocena, and Robert Bruno, all of whom are included in this volume.

The alternative film poster movement continues to thrive, with pieces selling at lightning-fast speeds via print houses and galleries such as Mondo, Skuzzles, Hero Complex, Bottleneck, Gallery 1988, Spoke Art, Grey Matter, and Dark City. The work of these film artists has also expanded rather quickly to ancillary products such as special edition Blu-ray packaging (Arrow, Scream Factory), film soundtracks (Waxwork, One Way Static), tees (Fright Rags), action figures (NECA, Mezco), and more.

Simultaneously, the movement is going even further underground. A sub-genre of alternative movie poster exists for one-of-a-kind private commissions, many of which are shown in the book. Forget limited poster runs in quantities of 100 or less; many fans are increasingly interested in editions of one.

I wanted to ensure that volumes one and two were as balanced as possible in terms of styles, genres, and countries of origin. However, one of the questions I heard most often was, "but where are the female designers?" For whatever reason, pop culture artwork does seem heavily lopsided toward the guys, and I invite more women to reach out for inclusion in a possible third edition. I will take this chance to spotlight some of my favorite female artists at the moment (all of whom are featured in this volume): Tracie Ching, Marie Bergeron, Erica Williams, Jessica Deahl, Marija Markovic, Mayra Fersner, Ridge Rooms, Sarah Collins of Lure Design, and of course the great Akiko Stehrenberger, who has been making a huge name for herself on both the underground and mainstream circuits. In addition, fifteen artists from the first volume were so popular with readers that they are making a second appearance here: Jason Edmiston, Gary Pullin, Matthew Esparza (Wonderbros), Jeremy Wheeler, Gregorz Domaradzki (Gabz), Dave Perillo, Anthony Petrie, James Gilleard, Lure Design, Chris Garofalo, Steve Dressler, CHOGRIN, Godmachine, Nathan Thomas Milliner, and Joshua Budich.

Where does this leave key art in the film industry? Mainstream posters are slowly (very slowly) coming around. Several of the artists in volume one have since been snapped up by studios for freelance gigs, and a few film houses are warming up to the idea of creating hand-drawn movie posters once again. But the stronghold still exists; studios can't get enough of using airbrushed celebrity head shots **rather than** artistic stand-alone pieces that command attention and convey some of the emotion from the film they represent.

So, a personal plea to the mainstream marketing machine in Hollywood. There's a multitude of enthusiastic artists in volume one and two just itching to jump on board. How about flipping through the book, choosing a style that might be a solid fit for one of your projects, and reaching out to one of the featured artists? Let's bring back that one-sheet magic of yesteryear.

I invite you to sit back and enjoy what could be for your favorite flicks. See you at the next convention, gallery show, in *Twenty-Four by Thirty-Six*, and possibly even in a book trilogy. Stay tuned for more.

–Matthew Chojnacki

Tracie Ching

LOCATION Washington, DC / US

SITE Tracieching.com

Dr. Strangelove
18 × 24 in (46 × 61 cm)

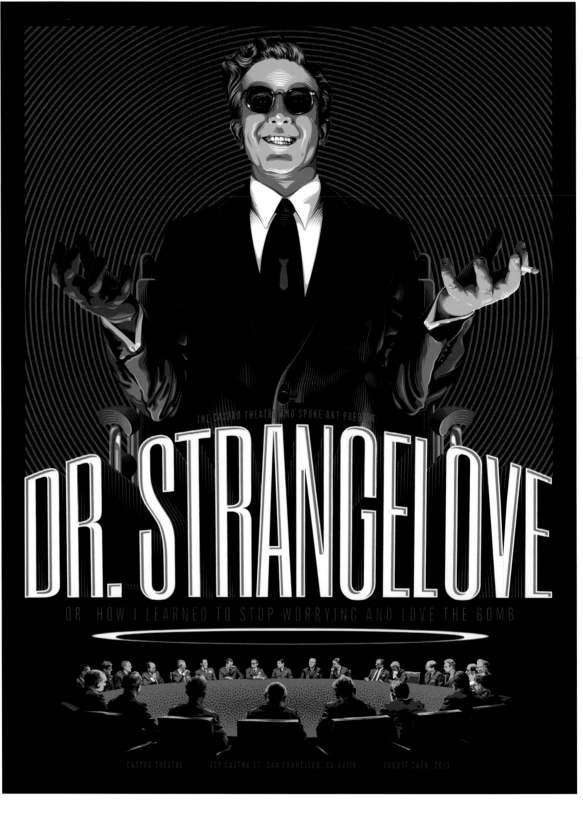

BEHIND THE POSTERS: *Dr. Strangelove*. In 2013, Spoke Art Gallery reached out about creating a print for a joint screening with San Francisco's historic Castro Theatre. They sent me Castro's lineup for the month of August and asked me to pick my favorites. I think Ken (owner of Spoke Art) was a little surprised when I immediately wrote back "Strangelove!" I have long been an avid Stanley Kubrick fan and felt that there was still a lot of room to create an iconic alternative silkscreen print, as *Dr. Strangelove* is often overlooked in favor of Kubrick's more popular films. To date it was one of my favorite subjects that I've had the pleasure of designing for.

2001: A Space Odyssey. In 2014, Spoke Art announced they were having an entire show dedicated to the work of Stanley Kubrick. I was ecstatic, as it meant a chance to expand my Kubrick prints into a set. I knew immediately that I wanted to tackle *2001: A Space Odyssey*, as it is my personal favorite among all of Kubrick's films. Even among contemporary science fiction, *2001* is still incredibly unique and inventive. I can only imagine what it was like sitting in a theater in 1968 and seeing Kubrick's stunning vision of our possible future.

INFLUENCES: Influences vary from project to project, but the longest-standing influence is my mother. She is an original fangirl and introduced me to my first film and television loves, particularly *Star Wars* and *Star Trek*. More than that, regardless of the job, topic, or client, I remember to work hard, work smart, and stay true to myself because of her.

FAVORITE FILM / GENRE: Science fiction, comedy, fantasy, drama (in that order). If you can find two or more of those things in a solid film, chances are I am going to *love* it.

FIRST FILM: I don't know for sure, but I can't remember a time when *Star Wars* wasn't part of my life. If I were a betting woman, that's where my money would be.

PREFERRED MEDIUM: Silkscreen and all other forms of printmaking.

CLIENTS: AMC, CBS, Sony Pictures, Google, Spoke Art Gallery.

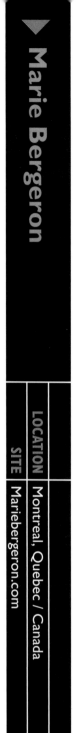

BEHIND THE POSTERS: *The Godfather* was created for the "I Am the Law / Law of Crime" show at Hero Complex Gallery. I really wanted to tackle an old classic that everybody adored. *The World's End* was commissioned for *ShortList* magazine, which is a great pop culture resource; it was also my first invitation from the magazine for a piece.

INFLUENCES: My influences come from a wide variety of artists, many of whom are not in the pop culture world: Pat Perry, Cleon Peterson, Erik Jones, Banksy, Obey, etc. In the film art culture, Olly Moss is probably at the top of my list. I am also heavily influenced by movies and video games. Kubrick's films, for example, have really inspired me.

FAVORITE FILM / GENRE: If I had to say one film, I would go with *American Beauty*. I love the script and think it's Kevin Spacey's best role. He just nailed it. Kubrick is very important for me as well. *The Shining*, *A Clockwork Orange*, and *2001: A Space Odyssey* are at the top of my list. I really miss Kubrick and his films.

FIRST FILM: Probably *Ace Ventura*. I fell in love with Ace when I was young! I also remember the first time my brother played *Alien* for me. I couldn't sleep for quite some time. What a great film.

THE
WORLD'S END
A FILM BY EDGAR WRIGHT

PREFERRED MEDIUM: I work digitally in Photoshop, from the initial sketches to the final piece. It gives me the chance to change anything in a single click. I also work on a Cintiq, which is a screen with pressure options—you can draw on it directly instead of having a graphic tablet and looking at a separate screen. It's the closest option to pencil and paper.

CLIENTS: I have a wide variety of clients, and am just beginning to get offers from the film industry. Paramount, Warner Bros., Fox, and Marvel have all recently expressed interest in purchasing my designs for use in promoting their films.

ADDITIONAL REMARKS: Most of my alternative posters were created for the Poster Posse, a group of twenty-plus artists who create alternative posters before a film is even released. It's basically for fun, but also to show big studios that artists can bring their film posters to another level. We started with just a few artists, whom we eventually tagged "the elite" (six of us), and then more came on board. The group is now better than ever, and recognition is everywhere.

From the depths of the sea...

A TIDAL WAVE OF TERROR!

ATTACK OF THE CRAB MONSTERS

starring
Richard GARLAND • Pamela DUNCAN • Russell JOHNSON
A ROGER CORMAN PRODUCTION • Screenplay by CHARLES B. GRIFFITH
Produced and Directed by ROGER CORMAN • AN ALLIED ARTISTS PICTURE

LITHO. IN U.S.A.

49633 57/115

BEHIND THE POSTERS: *Attack of the Crab Monsters.* I love classic B movies, and if the script demands that someone don a foam rubber suit and terrorize hapless victims (preferably of the bikini-clad variety), so much the better. *Attack of the Crab Monsters* has all of this and more, and the star of the movie, of course, is the eponymous creature itself. With its wildly flailing pincher claws barely under control by all-too-visible wires, and that wall-eyed humanoid face, you could almost feel sorry for the beast were it not for its ruthless plan to decimate the human population of the planet Earth. Working on this piece was such a blast that I plan on producing more images based on other movies of this genre, and because of the plethora of no-budget cinematic gems of the past, my goal to artistically honor as many of them as possible should keep me occupied for many years to come.

Dark Star. Growing up, my first experience with John Carpenter's *Dark Star* was within the pages of *Starlog* magazine, my viewing port on all things science fiction back then. The story of a jaded crew on a decades-long mission to blow up unstable planets with intelligent thermostellar bombs sent my imagination reeling. I remember seeing a picture of that simple wedge of a spaceship enveloped within an electromagnetic energy storm and immediately felt the compulsion to make a pencil drawing of it. This, to me, sounded like the best sci-fi movie since *Star Wars*' premiere a few months earlier, and I couldn't wait to see how Lt. Doolittle and the rest of his crew made out. But in a time before on-demand entertainment, the only option I had to view the film was the remote possibility of *Dark Star* coming to town for a midnight showing at the local movie revival house. It seemed that I had more of a chance of witnessing the "Phoenix Asteroids" than seeing this movie.

Dark Star
24 × 36 in (61 × 91 cm)

SCREAMFEST HORROR FILM FESTIVAL HONORS JOHN CARPENTER

Saturday, October 20th, 2012   Regal Cinemas L.A. Live Stadium 14, 1000 West Olympic Blvd., Los Angeles CA

It wouldn't be until a year or two later, when rifling through the back issues bins of Comic World in central California, that I would finally catch a glimpse of this soon-to-be cult classic playing on a wall-mounted television at the back of the shop. This was the moment I was waiting for. So I watched. I watched these bearded guys reluctantly embrace their collective ennui, confined by cardboard walls painted silver and held together with duct tape. I watched Pinback's life or death struggle with an alien "creature." And I watched Doolittle finally get his wish of surfing the waves into eternity. It wasn't anything like that tale from ". . . a galaxy far, far away," not by a long shot. But I loved it just the same.

So these many years later, when a friend contacted me to do a poster to honor the accomplishments of the horror master John Carpenter, I didn't hesitate in paying tribute to one of my favorite sci-fi movies of all time. Working on this piece took me right back to those days as a kid sitting at our living room coffee table, drawing that ill-fated spacecraft on its doomed mission in the great beyond.

PREFERRED MEDIUM: Due to my "day job" as an animation director, my time to work on personal projects can be very limited. That is why I produce all of my artwork digitally using various drawing and painting software to achieve the desired look. Because I worked with traditional media for many years, I apply the same thought processes and workflow to the digital realm to recreate the feel of traditional media. One of the best comments I receive is the surprise people express when they discover my work is digital, so I suppose the hard work is paying off.

The Exorcist
18 × 24 in (46 × 61 cm)

DESIGN FIRM	New Flesh
LOCATION	Austin, Texas / US
SITE	Newfleshprints.com

A **WILLIAM FRIEDKIN** FILM

WILLIAM PETER BLATTY'S

THE EXORCIST

WARNER BROS. PICTURES PRESENTS

WILLIAM PETER BLATTY'S "THE EXORCIST" DIRECTED BY WILLIAM FRIEDKIN ELLEN BURSTYN MAX VON SYDOW LEE J. COBB
KITTY WINN JACK MacGOWRAN JASON MILLER AS FATHER KARRAS LINDA BLAIR AS REGAN PRODUCED BY WILLIAM PETER BLATTY
EXECUTIVE PRODUCER NOEL MARSHALL SCREENPLAY BY WILLIAM PETER BLATTY BASED ON HIS NOVEL

POSTER BY NE

WARNER BROS. PICTURES
©2013 Warner Bros. Ent. All Rights Reserved

BEHIND THE POSTERS: I decided to do *The Exorcist* and *Night of the Living Dead* for two very different reasons. *The Exorcist* was created to commemorate the film's 40th anniversary. Somehow my work landed in front of director William Friedkin, who gave me the opportunity to create a new version of the poster. Friedkin seemed to be quite pleased with the results. He approved the print and even signed the variant edition.

The *Night of the Living Dead* print was my contribution to a horror-themed group show at Guzu Gallery here in Austin. When selecting a subject for a gallery show print, it is always important to create a piece that will both resonate with fans and sell. I always loved the raw nature of *Night of the Living Dead* and wanted to capture that in my illustration. Also, since the movie is in the public domain, it allowed me to legally include a billing block and title, which helped to elevate the piece from being an art print to more of a proper film poster.

INFLUENCES: I come from a cinematography background, so I have always been influenced by cinematographers like Jordan Cronenweth, Darius Khondji, Conrad Hall, and Roger Deakins. Film directors Ridley Scott, John Carpenter, David Fincher, and Akira Kurosawa are also huge influences because of their use of tone. When I am stuck and need inspiration I seem to always go back to the artwork of Drew Struzan, Jim Lee, Mike Mignola, and Tim Burton for a spark of creativity.

Night of the Living Dead
18 × 24 in (46 × 61 cm)

DESIGN FIRM	New Flesh
LOCATION	Austin, Texas / US
SITE	Newfleshprints.com

FAVORITE FILM / GENRE: I usually go with *Alien* or *Se7en*. If pressed I would probably say *Se7en*. The look of the film in combination with the direction, sound, and editing is just *too* good. I tend to gravitate toward films with a lot of atmosphere and strong visuals, so sci-fi is the obvious genre choice. *Star Wars*, *Alien*, and *Blade Runner* are my sweet spot. Also, I think it should be noted that all of these films could be considered a part of other genres. *Star Wars* could be a fantasy or "space opera," *Alien* is really a horror movie set in the future ("truckers in space"), etc. So, perhaps "atmosphere" would really be my favorite genre, if it were a genre.

FIRST FILM: *The Last Starfighter*. My parents took us to a drive-in and I remember being blown away. I still love that movie. There are just so many memorable lines in it.

PREFERRED MEDIUM: I love painting the most. However, there is something really satisfying about making screenprints. I print all of my own posters by hand and the process of mixing the inks and choosing the paper can really elevate the art into something special and different than originally envisioned. This is an overused statement, but you really have to see screenprints in person to appreciate them.

CLIENTS: I rarely do commercial work for companies directly, but I have created official prints for Marvel, MGM, Warner Bros., and Legendary Pictures. A good portion of the work I am currently completing is a backlog of commissions, along with a few gallery shows and official posters.

Tomasz Opasinski

Paris, je t'aime
27 × 40 in (69 × 102 cm)

DESIGN FIRM	ImageMassive, LLC
LOCATION	Los Angeles, California / US
SITE	Tomasz-opasinski.com

PARIS, JE T'AIME

2010

BEHIND THE POSTERS: I designed the original poster for *Paris Je T'aime* when it was released. Years later, I decided to revisit the idea with my own spin on the overall vibe of the poster.

With *The Thing*, I wanted to connect the title treatment with the story (to simplify the message). A few hours later, I was looking at finished artwork on my computer screen.

FAVORITE FILM / GENRE: Sci-fi, and of course *Aliens*.

The Thing
27 × 40 in (69 × 102 cm)

Tomasz Opasinski

DESIGN FIRM ImageMassive, LLC

LOCATION Los Angeles, California / US

SITE Tomasz-opasinski.com

FIRST FILM: I think it was a Russian cartoon, "Wilk i Zając," back in Poland, a looooooong time ago.

PREFERRED MEDIUM: Archival ink on canvas.

Jason Edmiston

Killer Klowns from Outer Space
24 × 36 in (61 × 91 cm)
A Skuzzles release

LOCATION Toronto / Canada

SITE Jasonedmiston.com

BEHIND THE POSTERS: Both were commissions from poster companies that had acquired licenses. I was approached by Skuzzles for *Killer Klowns* and by Gallery F for *The Texas Chainsaw Massacre*, as each company was aware of my previous horror poster work. Both films were visually interesting to me, so I jumped at the chance to work on pieces for them.

RECENT PROJECTS: The last year has been super varied. I have been working on a wide range of projects, from movie posters, toy packaging, magazine covers, vinyl album cover illustration, and resin art toys, to a handful of art gallery group shows and pop culture conventions. What I'm most satisfied with is probably my recent solo show at Mondo Gallery. "Movie Villains" was my theme for the exhibition, and it included original paintings, prints, and movie posters. It was a great success, selling out all screenprints and giclees (over 1,600 in all), as well as most of the 40+ acrylic paintings and pencil sketches.

THE TEXAS
CHAIN SAW
MASSACRE

A FILM BY TOBE HOOPER
40TH ANNIVERSARY PRESENTATION AT SXSW 2014
©MCMLXXIV by Vortex, Inc.

GALERIE F

POSTER BY JASON EDMISTON

PINCH ME MOMENT: I have run into a few celebrity collectors over the last few years, and I always get a thrill from it. I'm proud to say that directors Frank Darabont (*The Shawshank Redemption*) and Greg Nicatero (*Walking Dead*) own my work, as well as actor Robert Englund (Freddy Krueger) and musician Gerry Only (Misfits). I find that artists of all fields are fans themselves, and it's a fairly small professional world, so it makes sense that we'd all eventually cross paths.

IS THE FILM INDUSTRY COMING ALONG? I think art is cyclical by nature, so right now there is somewhat of a return to traditional illustration in movie posters and related genre art. Art directors want to stand out against the Photoshopped head shots that have become the standard, and that means that there is a lot more work for artists like me. Right now, this means more illustrated independent movie posters, but mainstream Hollywood is starting to take notice, too.

CLIENTS: Mondo, Fright Rags, Skuzzles, *Famous Monsters of Filmland*, *Rue Morgue*, NECA Toys.

ADDITIONAL REMARKS: I am having an incredible run right now. I'm getting to work on all of my dream projects and am having a blast doing it. Hopefully this run will last for a while.

Ben Bouchet

Lolita
23 × 33 in (59 × 84 cm)

LOCATION Paris / France

SITE Benbouchet.com

BEHIND THE POSTERS: Both posters were inspired by women. It's interesting to view these pieces side by side because they reflect different visions of women and their influences. *Lolita* has a very cynical side, showing fantasy through a man's eyes. It reflects a timeless concept, a deprived desire and forbidden fruit that dominate its male subject. I love the way Kubrick treated this topic.

   With *Cloclo*, I wanted to shed light on the almost mystical aura that surrounded French pop singer Claude François in the 1960s. Claude generated an absolute frenzy among women, who admired his music and dazzling success as an artist.

INFLUENCES: I am an unconditional fan of American print artists including Mikey Burton, DKNG, Aesthetic Apparatus, Invisible Creature, Jason Munn, etc. I also follow the work of Antoine et Manuel, M/M Paris, Laurent Fetis, and *Toilet Paper* magazine.

FAVORITE FILM / GENRE: I love French cinema, particularly from *La Nouvelle Vague* [the French new wave of the 1950s and 1960s]. Most recently I enjoyed *Saint Laurent* by Bertrand Bonello and *Mommy* by Xavier Dolan.

FIRST FILM: I have a very strong memory of *E.T.* by Steven Spielberg and *Le Grand Bleu* by Luc Besson. *Le Grand Bleu's* score (by Éric Serra) and Rosanna Arquette's superb leading performance fascinated me.

CLIENTS: I currently work as an in-house graphic designer for the brand Eleven Paris, which allows me to collaborate with large companies such as Urban Outfitters, ASOS, and Bloomingdale's. Thanks to Gallery 1988, I have also been able to show my artwork in the US.

PREFERRED MEDIUM: Anything allowing me to draw, starting with a pencil.

Friday the 13th
23 × 31 in (58 × 79 cm)
A Dark City Gallery release

LOCATION London / UK

SITE Dan-mumford.com

BEHIND THE POSTERS: I was asked by the excellent Dark City Gallery to work on these two pieces. I had previously collaborated with them on *The Evil Dead*, *Halloween*, and *The Fly*. *The Wicker Man* and *Friday the 13th* were back to back projects. *The Wicker Man* piece was very well-received, and over the course of six months became the official artwork for the film's re-release in cinemas and on DVD/Blu-ray. What a fantastic end to the project. Seeing my print turn into the official art for such a classic film was an amazing experience.

INFLUENCES: I try not to draw too much influence from other artists and do my own thing as much as possible. However, Marvel and DC artists from the 1990s–2000s formed an integral part of my youth. I was always trying to emulate these artists' styles as a kid, so they were a big influence on my art. I am also inspired by film directors, particularly Ridley Scott, Guillermo del Toro, and John Carpenter. The worlds they create resonate a lot with me, and I have always wanted to capture that in my work.

The Wicker Man
24 × 36 in (61 × 91 cm)
A Dark City Gallery release

LOCATION London / UK

SITE Dan-mumford.com

FAVORITE FILM / GENRE: My favorite film is probably *Aliens*, but it is closely tied with *Big Trouble in Little China* and *Blade Runner*. Completely different films, but all have amazing elements and qualities that continue to stick with me. My favorite genres are horror and sci-fi; anything that includes a fantastic new world will always draw me in. I struggle with films set in reality, instead preferring movies that bring me somewhere new and mysterious.

FIRST FILM: *Teenage Mutant Ninja Turtles* in 1990. I was five or six, and insisted that we sit in the front row. I thought it was amazing (and that Shredder was absolutely terrifying). Looking back, it is bizarrely dark for a film that is essentially aimed at kids.

PREFERRED MEDIUM: Unfortunately, digital. I say "unfortunately" as I think that it's a shame that I have moved away from traditional pen and ink. Digital arts give me more freedom, but at the same time I would prefer not to rely so much on technology. If I had more free time I would take up painting and try to flex my creative muscles in a new direction.

CLIENTS: Sony, Studio Canal, Red Bull, XBOX, Icon Motosports, Phish, Dark City Gallery, MGM, *Little White Lies*, Biffy Clyro, Gallows, Soundgarden, and many more.

Jaws 3-D
11 × 17 in (28 × 43 cm)

DESIGN FIRM	London 1888
LOCATION	Orlando, Florida / US
SITE	London1888.com

BEHIND THE POSTERS: I have been working with Mad Monster for a while, which includes creating posters for their screenings at the Chinese Theater in Hollywood. When they celebrated the anniversary of *Jaws 3-D*, Eben (of Mad Monster) asked me about doing a film poster similar to an old comic book 3-D. I had been wanting to use that idea for a while. *Jaws 3-D* was one of their biggest hit screenings, and the poster was a ton of fun to make. We eventually did a similar piece for *Friday the 13th 3-D*.

After doing those, I was approached by Pete from Spooky Empire. He was hosting a *Creature from the Black Lagoon* reunion at his convention. He wanted to have a 3-D *Creature* poster to commemorate that experience. This was another great success.

INFLUENCES: My biggest influences are composers. I listen to a lot of movie scores while drawing. It gets my brain moving. John Carpenter, Jerry Goldsmith, John Harrison. Also, I think my other artistic influence comes from 1980s horror movie lighting. *Creepshow*, *The Texas Chainsaw Massacre 2*, and Joe Dante films are my favorite examples.

DESIGN FIRM	London 1888
LOCATION	Orlando, Florida / US
SITE	London1888.com

CREATURE FROM THE BLACK LAGOON
RICHARD CARLSON JULIE ADAMS RICHARD DENNING
ANTONIO MORENO RICOU BROWNING written by HARRY ESSEX and
ARTHUR ROSS directed by JACK ARNOLD produced by WILLIAM ALLAND
poster by CHRISTOPHER OTT printed by JAKPRINTS

LONDON
1888

SPOOKY
EMPIRE

FAVORITE FILM / GENRE: Horror is definitely my favorite film genre. Favorite films include *Creepshow, The Texas Chainsaw Massacre, Big Trouble in Little China,* and *The Thing.*

FIRST FILM: The first film I ever saw in the theater was *E.T.* I also remember seeing *Ghostbusters* in the theater several times at a young age.

PREFERRED MEDIUM: I mainly work digitally. I will sketch ideas/compositions on paper, and then drop them into the computer and ink over them with my Wacom tablet.

CLIENTS: Mad Monster, NECA, Kirk Hammett, Spooky Empire, Rock and Shock.

DESIGN FIRM Akikomatic, LLC
LOCATION Los Angeles, California / US
SITE Akikomatic.com

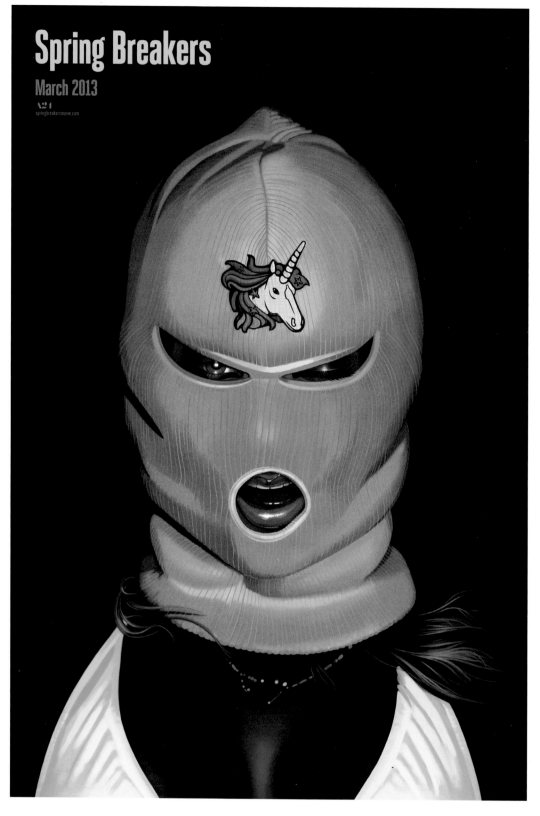

Spring Breakers
27 × 40 in (69 × 102 cm)

Spring Breakers
March 2013
A24
springbreakersmovie.com

BEHIND THE POSTERS: Commissioned by A24, I presented a few different poster ideas for *Spring Breakers*. The mask (shown here) was the only illustrated design. I wanted to play off the fluorescent and neon colors that are prominent throughout the film, and I thought that this particular image effectively summarized sex, youth, and crime. Also, I chose this particular illustration style because I felt it needed to be slick to feel appropriate to the film.

Regarding *Her*, Spike Jonze films always give room for unconventional visual content. I thought the image shown here would be a surreal way to communicate the woman in the protagonist's ear/mind without showing either of the two characters' likenesses. Also, I thought that using black and white would feel timeless, yet modern.

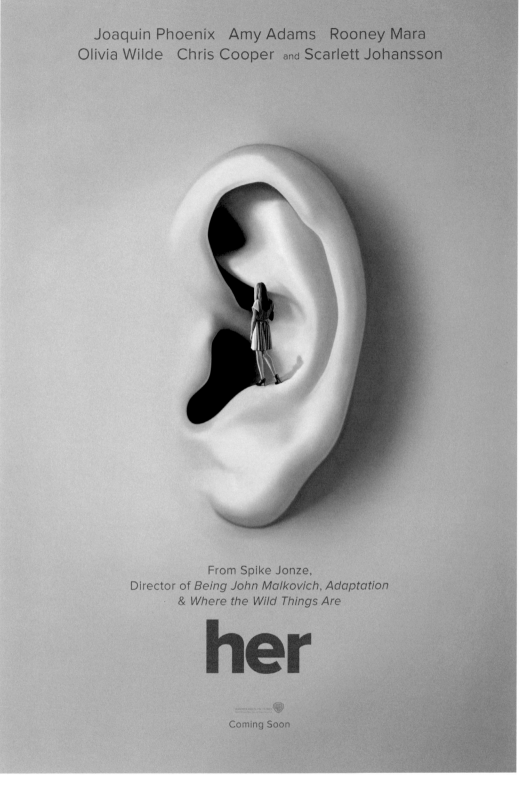

Joaquin Phoenix   Amy Adams   Rooney Mara
Olivia Wilde   Chris Cooper and Scarlett Johansson

From Spike Jonze,
Director of *Being John Malkovich*, *Adaptation*
& *Where the Wild Things Are*

her

Coming Soon

INFLUENCES: For movie poster projects I draw inspiration from so many different areas. Overall I feel it is important that the look and feel of the poster be as well-considered as the content in the image. I do not believe in designing a random style of illustration just for illustration's sake. All of the visual pieces have to fit together appropriately or else the artist isn't doing what he or she is hired to do, which is sell and communicate a first glimpse of the film.

FAVORITE FILM / GENRE: Horror, art house, documentary, comedy.
FIRST FILM: *The Dark Crystal.*
CLIENTS: A24, A&E, FX, Oscilloscope Laboratories, Radius/TWC, T/F Fest, Weiden + Kennedy, Zeitgeist Films.
PREFERRED MEDIUM: Acrylic.

BEHIND THE POSTERS: *Night of the Demons* has been an all-time favorite since I first watched it. It's exactly the type of movie that I love, with its terrible acting, corny special effects, and overall camp value. It has become a movie that I watch every Halloween season, and I have made every one of my friends watch it (including my girlfriend). Strange Kids Club came to me with an opportunity to design a poster for them, and it just so happened that we were both huge fans of *Night of the Demons*. It was also the 30th anniversary of the film, so this was our tribute to that amazing flick.

The Toxic Avenger was a movie that I was always aware of, but never watched until high school. However, I remember as a kid catching the cartoon version of the movie, *Toxic Crusaders*, and even had a few action figures from the show. So when Troma put out their first "Tox Box" *Toxic Avenger* movie set, I grabbed it. I must admit, when I first watched the movie I thought it was one of the worst films ever made. I decided to give it another try, this time with one of my best friends. The second time was so much better, as we were cracking jokes throughout the entire movie. I was then hooked and it jumped onto my favorites list. When Bottleneck Gallery was doing a cult movie art show, I decided to offer *The Toxic Avenger*. This poster was heavily influenced by old skateboard art from the 1980s, homaging a Santa Cruz Rob Roskopp skateboard that came out the same year as *The Toxic Avenger*, 1984.

INFLUENCES: Frank Frazetta has always been one of my favorite artists. I was a big 1990s comic nerd when I was a kid, so Jim Lee had a huge impact on me. I was also obsessed with *Ninja Turtles*, and as an adult discovered the comic books, so Eastman and Laird were influences. Skateboard artists like Jim Phillips, VCJ, Marc Mckee, and Sean Cliver were some of my favorites. When it comes to movies, John Carpenter is at the top. Plus, let's not forget Saturday morning cartoons like *The Real Ghostbusters*, *Batman: The Animated Series*, and a lot of the Hanna-Barbera cartoons.

FIRST FILM: The first ones that made the biggest impact on me would be *The Neverending Story*, *3 Ninjas*, and the first *Ninja Turtles* movie.
PREFERRED MEDIUM: I have worked digitally for the past six or seven years.
CLIENTS: Gallery 1988, Bottleneck Gallery, Spoke Art Gallery, Fright Rags, Burton, Mishka, 10 Deep, *Front* magazine.

Gary Pullin

The Howling
18 × 24 in (46 × 61 cm)

LOCATION Toronto, Ontario / Canada

SITE Garypullin.com

A FILM BY JOE DANTE

BEHIND THE POSTERS: *The Howling* was created for Hero Complex Gallery's "Kings of Cult: A Tribute to Joe Dante and Roger Corman." The concept of hiding the title in the fur of the transforming wolf was a quick idea at the start of the project. Adam Smasher was great to work with at Hero and I was honored to be included in the show.

Fright Night was created with my friends at Poster Collective. I presented several concepts, but we agreed to think outside the box on this one. The image is inspired by the opening shot of the film, where the camera swoops up to Charley Brewster's bedroom window while Peter Vincent's *Fright Night* television show is broadcasting. The viewer becomes the voyeur,

the vampire at the window, watching Peter Vincent on *Fright Night*. I had a lot of fun hiding elements from the film in the poster, such as garlic and a pencil, which both became resourceful tools against vampires in the flick.

RECENT PROJECTS: I recently created key art and a Mondo poster for *The Babadook*. I really love working on vinyl horror soundtracks, too. It merges my love of films and music into one awesome package, and it's a lot of fun reinterpreting the art. It's like working on a film poster in the way that you have to create a captivating image for the film, but additionally you want to capture the atmosphere and style of the music or composer. The large-size format of LPs, plus the gatefolds, center labels,

28

Fright Night
18 × 24 in (46 × 61 cm)
A Poster Collective release

LOCATION Toronto, Ontario / Canada

SITE Garypullin.com

die-cuts, and the vinyl record itself allows artists to create fun concepts that we can incorporate into the design. You're not only creating two-dimensional artwork with LPs, you're creating an extra dimension for the listener to experience.

PINCH ME MOMENT: It is a big thrill when art blogs, film sites, or books (like this one) ask to publish my work! I was also recently featured in *Entertainment Weekly* and on Movies.com for *The Babadook* poster. And I love when fans get my work tattooed. It's the ultimate compliment, and becomes a very personal connection between the artist and the person getting inked.

IS THE FILM INDUSTRY COMING ALONG? Lately it seems that studios have been paying more attention and taking risks with their designs. This is not only because of the artists, but also due to poster houses like Skuzzles and Mondo. I think that the "art" behind poster design is really returning in a huge way, and it continues to gain momentum. I'm glad that it is starting to resonate within the big studio system, but I am just as happy that it is connecting with television companies, independent film studios, directors, writers, and collectors. We'll keep it alive. I have no worries there.

CLIENTS: Mondo, Waxwork Records, Death Waltz Records, Skuzzles, MGM, IFC, CBS.

One Flew Over the Cuckoo's Nest
18 × 24 in (46 × 61 cm)

LOCATION New England / US

SITE Seekandspeak.com

FRIDAY NIGHT FILM SERIES · 7:00 PM IN THE LARGE MEETING ROOM · ASHLAND PUBLIC LIBRARY
SUPPORTED BY THE FRIENDS OF THE ASHLAND PUBLIC LIBRARY AND AUDIENCE DONATIONS · FREE AND OPEN TO ALL

BEHIND THE POSTERS: In late-2008 I was looking for a personal project to work on during my free time, and got the idea to make my own posters for films after seeing a flyer hanging at my local library for a film series they ran every Friday night. My job at the time involved designing brochures for biomedical equipment, so I was looking for an outlet that was more creative and aligned more toward my interests. Most of the films I chose came from recalling what I'd seen over the years; the research was already done, and I could get started right away. *One Flew Over the Cuckoo's Nest* and *1984* were two of many that popped up instantly.

INFLUENCES: Bob Gill might be my favorite designer. At the end of the day, he's more concerned with what something says rather than how it looks. I'm not as sharp as others when it comes to craft, but I can find a way in to most problems by thinking of an idea, so his approach has always resonated with me. Tony Palladino is another artist cut from the same cloth. And then there's Barbara "Basha" Baranowska whose approach is the complete opposite, but who has created some of the most jaw-dropping film art around.

LOCATION New England / US

SITE Seekandspeak.com

GEORGE ORWELL

"WAR IS PEACE. FREEDOM IS SLAVERY. IGNORANCE IS STRENGTH."

FAVORITE FILM / GENRE: I have an unhealthy fondness for movies from the 1980s. They're just incredibly charming.
FIRST FILM: *Young Einstein* is the first film that I can clearly remember cutting the ads out of the paper for. It was all downhill from there.
PREFERRED MEDIUM: Whatever gets the job done. All finished work winds up going through the computer, though.

CLIENTS: Unzero Films, Drafthouse Films, Tribeca Film, Oscilloscope Laboratories, IFC Films, Eureka! Entertainment, Park Circus Films, Sony, MGM, Warner Bros., *The New York Times*. I have also handled the official key-art for theatrical re-releases of a few classic films, including *Whatever Happened to Baby Jane?* and *Lawrence of Arabia*.
ADDITIONAL REMARKS: San Dimas High School Football Rules?

The Blues Brothers
24 × 36 in (61 × 91 cm)

CAPACITY
18 PERSONS

NO SMOKING

LOCATION Tolentino (MC) / Italy

SITE Sketchesnatched.blogspot.it

BEHIND THE POSTERS: All of my pieces are born from the passion that I have for cinema, and often depict aspects of a film that in some way have marked a historical point for filmmaking. They also typically correspond with my personal tastes, as is the case here with John Landis' *The Blues Brothers* and David Lynch's *Elephant Man*.

INFLUENCES: My artistic influences are endless and it is difficult to make a list. A brief selection would include painters such as Sargent, Zorn, Boldini, the whole period of realism, and also the most successful of artists such as Rockwell, Fawcett, Sickles, and Bernie Fuchs. Regarding comic illustrators: Toth, Breccia, Zaffino, Bernet, Sienkiewicz and countless others.

FAVORITE FILM / GENRE: I don't have a favorite genre, but if I have to pick a single film, perhaps *2001: A Space Odyssey.* Favorite directors include Kubrick, Lynch, Hitchcock, Coppola, Herzog, Malick, and many more.

PREFERRED MEDIUM: Acrylic and watercolor.
CLIENTS: I currently work in Italy, mainly with Italian comic publisher Sergio Bonelli Editore.

A Grand Day Out
24 × 36 in (61 × 91 cm)

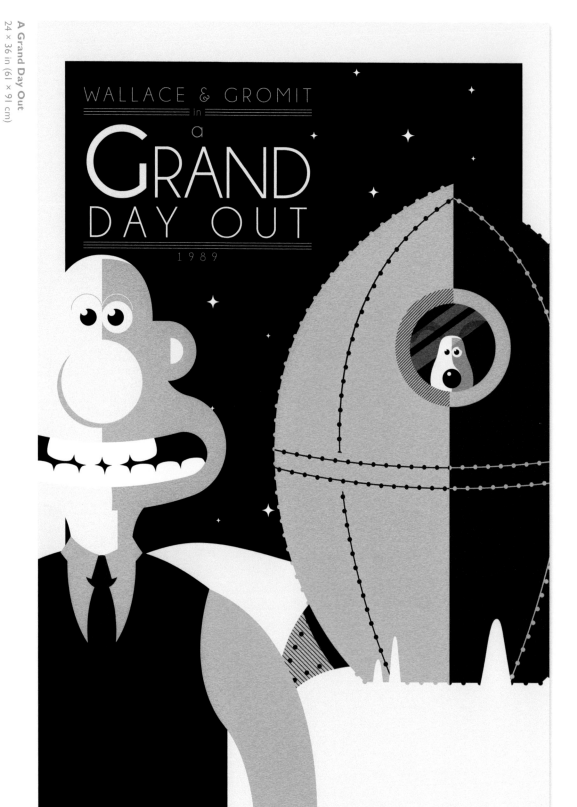

WALLACE & GROMIT
in
a
GRAND
DAY OUT
1989

ALIAS UNIQ

LOCATION Columbus, Ohio / US

SITE Uniqdesign.net

BEHIND THE POSTERS: *Wallace and Gromit* was the first poster I ever created. I grew up watching *Wallace and Gromit* and it has always been very special to me. In grade school I even nicknamed a younger kid that I was friends with "Gromit" because of our close friendship. I created the *Bebe's Kids* poster for a media company that saw my previous work.

INFLUENCES: My biggest influences would be Nick Bertke (Pogo), Tom Whalen (Strongstuff), WinterArtwork, Amanda Flagg, and Kari Fry. My favorite film directors are Hayao Miyazaki, Chris Columbus, and John Hughes.

FAVORITE FILM / GENRE: My all-time favorite movie is *The Lion King*. I could watch animated movies or comedies all day.

Bebe's Kids
24 × 36 in (61 × 91 cm)
A DzXtinKt Originals release

ALIAS	UNIQ
LOCATION	Columbus, Ohio / US
SITE	Uniqdesign.net

FIRST FILM: The first film that I can remember seeing in the theater was *Aladdin*. Although, I'm not quite sure if it counts, because the sequence with the sand tiger scared me so much that I hid under my jacket and ended up falling asleep.

PREFERRED MEDIUM: I love all forms of digital art and have tried my hand at almost every form there is. However, I prefer to stick with vector illustrations and photo manipulations in Illustrator and Photoshop, respectively.

CLIENTS: I'm still working on getting my name out there. DzXtinKt Originals was the first on board.

ADDITIONAL REMARKS: There is no life I know to compare with pure imagination.

Beetlejuice
28 × 39 in (70 × 100 cm)

LOCATION Torino / Italy

SITE Vanortondesign.com

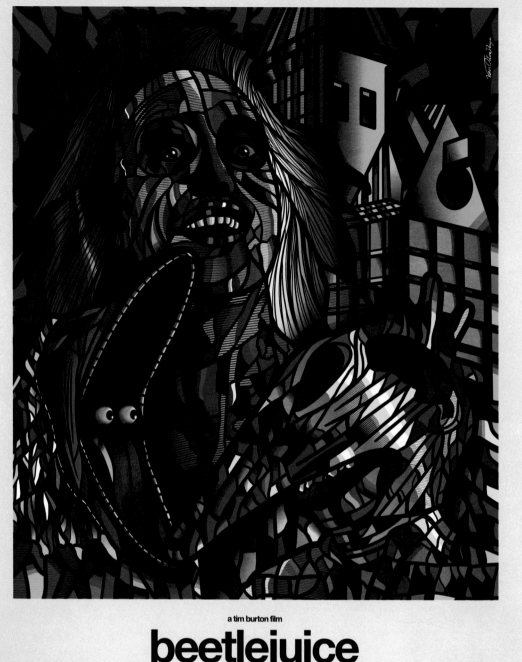

a tim burton film

beetlejuice

michael keaton   **alec baldwin**   **geena davis**

starring alec baldwin • geena davis • michael keaton • jeffrey jones • catherine o'hara • winona ryder
music by danny elfman • director of photography thomas ackerman • story by michael mcdowell & larry wilson
produced by michael bender larry wilson and richard hashimoto • directed by tim burton

BEHIND THE POSTERS: We generally focus on 1980s movies and felt that these two films in particular were quite visionary. *RoboCop* really pushed the sense of imagination with its style, while *Beetlejuice* was a dark, visual film that really popped for us.
INFLUENCES: We are influenced by all of Dario Argento's films. Argento creates an incredible mix of stunning coloring with a fantastic geometric aesthetic. In terms of poster artists, La Boca is incredible.

FAVORITE FILM / GENRE: Favorite films, in random order, include *Cinema Paradiso*, *The Game*, *The Shawshank Redemption*, *Deep Red*, and many more.

a paul verhoeven film

robocop

peter weller

starring peter weller • nancy allen • robocop • daniel o'herlihy
director of photography jost vacano • film editor frank j.urioste • music by basil poleidorus
written by edward neumeier & michael miner • produced by arne schmidt • directed by paul verhoeven

Van Orton Design

LOCATION	Torino / Italy
SITE	Vanortondesign.com

PREFERRED MEDIUM: We make digital art, primarily using a Wacom tablet and Photoshop.
CLIENTS: *Rolling Stone* Italy, Spoke Art Gallery, Hero Complex Gallery.

ADDITIONAL REMARKS: Other films that we have created film posters for include *Back to the Future, Blade Runner, Gremlins, Big, Big Trouble in Little China, Terminator, Batman, The Goonies, E.T., Ghostbusters, Star Wars*, and others. This list can go on and on, because the number of potential 1980s cult films is endless.

Saving Private Ryan
18 × 24 in (46 × 61 cm)

DESIGN FIRM	Bruno Digital Illustration
LOCATION	Brooklyn, New York / US
SITE	Brunodi.com

BEHIND THE POSTERS: *Saving Private Ryan* was created for the "Imagined Worlds" show at the Hero Complex Gallery. The show paid tribute to several prominent Hollywood directors and their works. One of the selected directors was Steven Spielberg. On a side note, *Saving Private Ryan* has always been one of my all-time favorite films. As hard as it is to watch, I've never been more impacted by the relationships between characters, and in this case the bond between soldiers. A true masterpiece. I remember seeing *Indiana Jones* when I was a little kid and being incredibly intrigued. Aside from loving the actual film, I also remember being blown away by the artwork, particularly the posters by Drew Struzan. This piece was my personal tribute to both the *Indiana Jones* franchise and Drew's incredible posters for the films.

INFLUENCES: Having been fortunate enough to study at Pratt Institute (thanks, Dad) I was required to take many art history courses and was engulfed with the paintings of the masters throughout the centuries. Rembrandt and Caravaggio served as my early painting inspirations, and then when I branched off to concentrate on illustration, Drew Struzan and Bob Peak were influential in developing my style and technique.

I was also influenced by film at a young age. I loved the storytelling and relationships between characters that a director was able to develop in just two hours. I knew early on that I wanted to create visual depictions of these characters. There is such an "art" and compelling nature of telling the story of a film in one poster.

Indiana Jones and the Last Crusade
18 × 24 in (46 × 61 cm)

Robert Bruno

DESIGN FIRM Bruno Digital Illustration
LOCATION Brooklyn, New York / US
SITE Brunodi.com

FAVORITE FILM / GENRE: I love drama and historical films. Choosing a favorite is always tough. It would probably be a tie between *Gladiator* and the *The Godfather Part II*.

FIRST FILM: When I was young, my mother took me to see a lot of the big Disney films as they came out. Although I enjoyed all of them, *The Lion King* really sticks out in my mind. For that genre, it was an unusually mature, complex film that delivered powerful messages and morals throughout.

PREFERRED MEDIUM: Graphite for sketches and rough comps and then digital media (Photoshop) for coloring and painting.

CLIENTS: I split my time between both pop culture/film-based clients and sports illustration. Some notable clients include Marvel, Philadelphia Eagles, Miami Dolphins, University of Central Florida, Intermedia Outdoors, Hero Complex Gallery, and Gallery 1988.

ADDITIONAL REMARKS: Over the last few years, I have been thrilled to see a massive resurgence in the illustrated poster world. Mondo, Hero Complex Gallery, and groups like the Poster Posse are creating incredible artwork that often rival and surpass the "official" film posters. I look forward to seeing this movement grow more in the near future.

Death Proof
12 × 16 in (30 × 41 cm)

DESIGN FIRM Wonderbros

LOCATION Planet Houston / US

SITE Wonderbros.com

BEHIND THE POSTERS: My brother Mike came up with the classic video game idea. *Death Proof* and *Planet Terror* were part of a series created for a Tarantino-themed art show. I initially sketched out some comps and showed them to Mike, who mentioned that I should "make them look like old Nintendo covers." Funny . . . he's had the same idea for *several* projects since.

RECENT PROJECTS: I am always working on new poster designs. Since *Alternative Movie Posters* volume one I have illustrated book covers for a few authors and designed a campaign for a touring musical. I'm working on many private commissions and a few independent films: *Burn in Hell!* and *Movie Night*, plus the documentary *Muse of Fire*.

Matthew Esparza

Death Proof
12 × 16 in (30 × 41 cm)

DESIGN FIRM: Wonderbros
LOCATION: Planet Houston / US
SITE: Wonderbros.com

PINCH ME MOMENT: A girl on Instagram posted a tattoo of *The Thing* based on my poster design. Wonderbros also recently had a booth at a Comic Con in 2014. It was our first time selling work at a convention, and the response was overwhelming. It's such an awesome feeling seeing someone light up a smile when they flip through your portfolio.

IS THE FILM INDUSTRY COMING ALONG? You can't judge a film by its poster. However, posters are just as important as anything else selling the film. Posters and nachos.

CLIENTS: Time Bomb Pictures, Blood Flood Productions, Don Roff, Marilyn Vance.

ADDITIONAL REMARKS: I'm a big fan of this book series. I've had the opportunity of meeting and chatting with some of the artists from volume one. It's a pleasure to share these pages with such raw and humble talent.

Paul Shipper

Guardians of the Galaxy
27 × 40 in (69 × 102 cm)

DESIGN FIRM Paul Shipper Studio

LOCATION South West England / UK

SITE Paulshipper.com

BEHIND THE POSTERS: I simply could not resist giving Marvel's *Guardians of the Galaxy* the illustrated poster treatment. I created this print before the movie was released, when reference sources were thin on the ground. I was happy with how it turned out. For *The Hobbit* I simply wanted to draw Gandalf again. I sketched it on my iPad and made it available as a Christmas present to my fans the year it was released.

INFLUENCES: For me, the big four have always been Drew Struzan, Richard Amsel, J. C. Leyendecker, and Norman Rockwell. I am influenced by many more—many of whom are my contemporaries.
FAVORITE FILM / GENRE: Sci-fi, action/adventure, thriller.
FIRST FILM: *The Jungle Book*.

The Hobbit
27 × 40 in (69 × 102 cm)

DESIGN FIRM	Paul Shipper Studio
LOCATION	South West England / UK
SITE	Paulshipper.com

PREFERRED MEDIUM: Traditional—acrylic airbrush / Prismacolor pencils. Digital—Wacom/Photoshop/ SketchBook Pro
CLIENTS: Disney, CBS, IDW, Gravillis Inc., Magnolia Pictures, *The Sunday Times*, JWT, Lucasfilm, Intrada, Penguin Books, Topps, AMC, Child Helpline International, *GQ*, Riot Games, Miramax, MGM, FOX, HBO, Shout Factory, Anchor Bay, Bonnier Corp.

ADDITIONAL REMARKS: Paul's artwork has been appreciated by key players in the film industry, including J. J. Abrams, Edgar Wright, Simon Pegg, Tom Hanks, Tom Tykwer, and the Wachowski siblings.

Studiohouse Designs

The Goonies
19 × 25 in (48 × 64 cm)

DESIGNERS | Kevin Thomas & Cody Brown
LOCATION | Pennsylvania / US
SITE | Studiohousedesigns.com

BEHIND THE POSTERS: In June 2014 we were scheduled to vend at the Bizarre AC horror con [New Jersey] where three big reunions were scheduled: *Hellraiser, The Lost Boys,* and *The Goonies.* After talking with the promoter, we learned that our good friend Chris Garofalo was already creating a print for *The Lost Boys,* so Cody and I chose to do posters for *The Goonies* and *Hellraiser.* For both pieces we wanted the images to have an elegant, gothic look to them. I [Kevin] have always wanted to create a *Goonies* poster, but it was selfish decision on my end to do it in conjunction with Bizarre AC, because I figured I could possibly use it to meet the cast. For *Hellraiser,* I had the idea for the box as the upside-down cross, but my favorite detail is Cody's mice impaled by nails. Look closely. They are hidden in plain sight, yet no one ever notices them.

INFLUENCES: Kevin: Aaron Horkey, Paul Shipper, and Tracie Ching (she's our friend, but Tracie is so good that it makes me want to up my game). Tim Burton's art was also a huge influence growing up. Cody: Matt Taylor, Florian Bertmer, Josh Smith (aka Hydro74), Nicholas Delort, and Daniel Danger.

FAVORITE FILM / GENRE: Kevin: *Star Wars* is my favorite film, but I grew up having an undying love for the classic Universal monster films, as well as watching all of the terrible horror movie marathons on [cable station] USA throughout the late '80s and '90s. Cody: My fondest memory is stealing my mother's copy of *Hellraiser* and sneaking it up to my room. I remember shitting my pants because it was so scary. My dad got me into *Star Wars* trilogy when I was around seven.

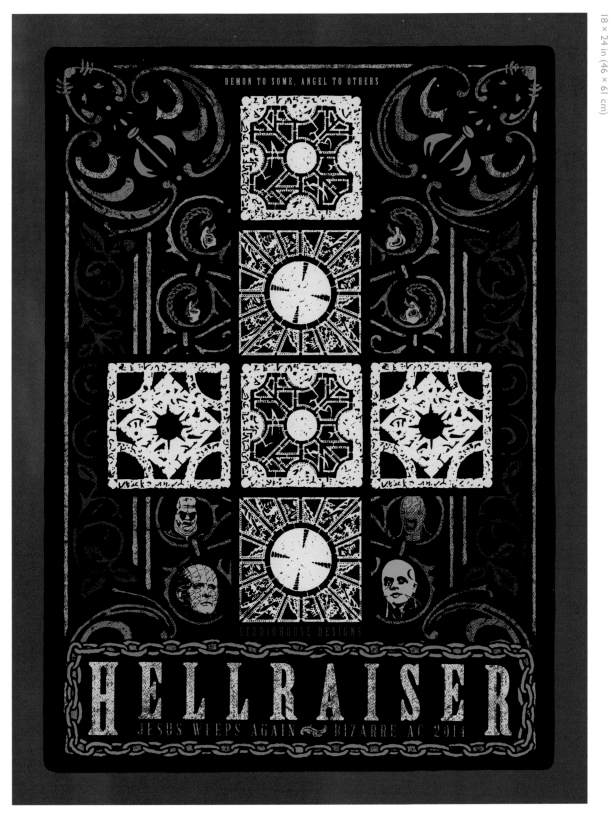

Hellraiser
18 × 24 in (46 × 61 cm)

DESIGNERS	Kevin Thomas & Cody Brown
LOCATION	Pennsylvania / US
SITE	Studiohousedesigns.com

FIRST FILM: Kevin: The *Star Wars* trilogy was the first movie that I became obsessed with. I wore out many VHS copies of each film throughout my childhood. Growing up, my dad and I watched so many films together that he would test me on *Star Wars* actors and what else they had been in. Cody: The first film that I remember being obsessed with was *Teenage Mutant Ninja Turtles*. TMNT played a huge role in my childhood. As far as quality films, *Back to the Future*. I remember watching it all the time and pretending that I was Marty McFly. My dad was Doc Brown and we would fly back in time and go on sweet adventures.
CLIENTS: Hero Complex Gallery, The Alternative Gallery, *Fangoria*, *Starlog*, *Gore Noir*, Cold Cuts Clothing, Jay & Brian's Excellent Video Store.

ADDITIONAL REMARKS: Kevin: I want to thank our families for tolerating the long hours we put into this. Also thanks to Chris Garofalo for the initial push to "just go for it," and to James Heimer, an old friend whom I have annoyed more than anyone with business and technique-based questions. Cody: Thanks to Kevin for getting me into the world of designing and printing posters, Chris Garofalo for letting me bug him with questions at all hours, and my best friends, Andy Morris and Jeff Sotace, for pushing me to not be a shitty artist. Also, to my wonderful girlfriend, Erin Jacob, for always supporting me. If it weren't for these people, I would not be able to pursue this dream.

Lost in Translation
18 × 24 in (46 × 61 cm)

BILL MURRAY   SCARLETT JOHANSSON
In an American Zoetrope / Elemental Films Production
Lost In Translation
co-starring
Giovanni Ribisi / Anna Faris / Fumihiro Hayashi
Produced by Ross Katz and Sofia Coppola / Executive Producer Francis Ford Coppola and Fred Roos / Written and Directed by Sofia Coppola
Technicolor / Production Designer Anne Ross and K.K. Barrett / Editor Sarah Flack / Suggested for Mature Audiences

BEHIND THE POSTERS: *Lost in Translation* was a private commission from a group of avid poster collectors. They wanted me to create a poster for a film that they felt hadn't been served well yet with a print. They gave me a list of potential candidates and *Lost in Translation* jumped out at me, as it's a favorite of mine. *The Graduate* poster was produced for Grey Matter Art. We spent a couple of months going back and forth to see what was a good fit, but as soon as they obtained the license for *The Graduate* the search was over.

INFLUENCES: Paul Pope is at the top of the list. The energy in his work is incredible.
FAVORITE FILM / GENRE: It is difficult to narrow it down to just one, but I have watched *Almost Famous* more times than I can remember.

The Graduate
18 × 24 in (46 × 61 cm)
A Grey Matter Art release

LOCATION Chichester, Sussex / United Kingdom

SITE Matttaylor.co.uk

FIRST FILM: Either *E.T.* or *Return of the Jedi.*
PREFERRED MEDIUM: I love designing for screen printing. There's no other technique that allows you the vibrancy of color, yet limiting your palette leads to some bold and interesting design choices.

CLIENTS: Some of the highlights: Penguin Books, Mondo, Burton Snowboards, *The Washington Post*, Adidas.

Dawn of the Planet of the Apes
18 × 24 in (46 × 61 cm)

DESIGN FIRM	Mexifunk
LOCATION	East Coast / US
SITE	Mexifunk.com

BEHIND THE POSTERS: I have idle hands and a crazy imagination that doesn't rest. Also, being a member of the Poster Posse, at times certain movie titles will become a point of interest for either a group tribute or an individual tribute. *Dawn* was an individual vector tribute. When I created the print I had not yet seen the movie, but had grown up with the Charlton Heston originals, so I couldn't resist. Adobe featured it as "The Best of Behance." With the *X-Men* vector, the Poster Posse had already released its "phase 1" and "phase 2" tributes for this movie, but at the time I had just joined the artist group, so I caught up and created the poster seen here.

INFLUENCES: Sci-fi, fantasy, pop art, N. C. Wyeth, Bob Peak, Basquiat, Russian constructivists, futurism, art deco, graffiti, John Singer Sargent, Hokusai, Masamune Shirow, Katsuhiro Otomo, Bruce Lee, culture, science, the female form, and art history.

Orlando Arocena

DESIGN FIRM	Mexifunk
LOCATION	East Coast / US
SITE	Mexifunk.com

FAVORITE FILM / GENRE: *Infernal Affairs, Adventures of Baron Munchausen, Enter the Dragon.*
FIRST FILM: *Enter the Dragon.*
PREFERRED MEDIUM: Vector

CLIENTS: Adobe, Wacom, Jose Cuervo Tequila, New York International Auto Show, Hewlett Packard (HP), *The Wall Street Journal*, PepsiCo, and design agencies up and down I-95.

Jeremy Wheeler

Creepshow
18 × 24 in (46 × 61 cm)

DESIGN FIRM Bang! Media

LOCATION Ann Arbor, Michigan / US

SITE Thisisbangmedia.com

BEHIND THE POSTERS: Both were created for shows at Hero Complex Gallery—an amazing place run by amazing people who support amazing art. *Creepshow* was for the "King for a Day" tribute to Stephen King. Other than that flick bein' the bee's knees, its unique use of color screamed for a blacklight print, and the fine folks at VGKIDS came through with the printing. *Death Race 2000* was for the "Kings of Cult" tribute to Joe Dante and Roger Corman. It's been my favorite movie since I was young. I tried to connect my art to the many amazing ads that already existed for *Death Race 2000*. My logo, for example, was based on the Turkish poster title, and Frankenstein's angled car is very much like the one in the Japanese poster (a topic I know too well if you check out my Ignite talk on YouTube). As for the colors, I wanted them to be bright and bold, just like the film.

Again, VGKIDS did a great job with printing two split fountains with high-energy inks that sear into your brain. The idea was to always go big with the size. Go big or go home. As Junior Bruce would say, "All right, all right, and yes-sirree!"

RECENT PROJECTS: Be on the lookout for Blue Snaggletooth's second LP, *Beyond Thule*, for which I've drawn the gatefold art. It was designed so that the LPs make a continuous image when you put them next to each other, which is pretty unique and damned cool! Other than that, there's a big Blu-ray cover in the UK on the horizon. Though low on movie-related content, the comic I made for *The Ann* magazine about gentrification in Ann Arbor is pretty interesting and well worth looking up, since it echoes a lot of other budding cities' problems at the moment. Future comics will see me continue

Death Race 2000
24 × 36 in (61 × 91 cm)

DESIGN FIRM	Bang! Media
LOCATION	Ann Arbor, Michigan / US
SITE	Thisisbangmedia.com

to cover movie tie-in novelizations—an untapped source of fascinating movie merch that I can't get enough of. Look for that on a website soon.

PINCH ME MOMENT: An amazing thing about fandom is how your work can get in front of the original filmmaker's eyes—from William Friedkin to George A. Romero to Albert Maysles to John Carpenter. Seeing pics of my work with these giants gets me mad pumped and proud.

IS THE FILM INDUSTRY COMING ALONG? There are hints of hope out there, especially in indie cinema and DVD/Blu-ray packaging, but traditional campaigns continue to rule the day. Still, you can't deny the rabid popularity of revival art, whether for posters, soundtracks, art shows, what-have-you. They'd be smart to tap into it more (as long as they pay for it).

CLIENTS: Death Waltz Records, FrightFest Originals, *Esquire*, *A.V. Club*, The Bang! Dance Party, DUO, AADL, Blue Snaggletooth, Vault of Midnight, VGKIDS.

ADDITIONAL REMARKS: Honestly, I just can't wait to see this second volume. There's so much talent out there. Thanks for all of the support. Hope you dig these two pieces as much as I dug makin' 'em!

Total Recall
17 × 23 in (42 × 59 cm)

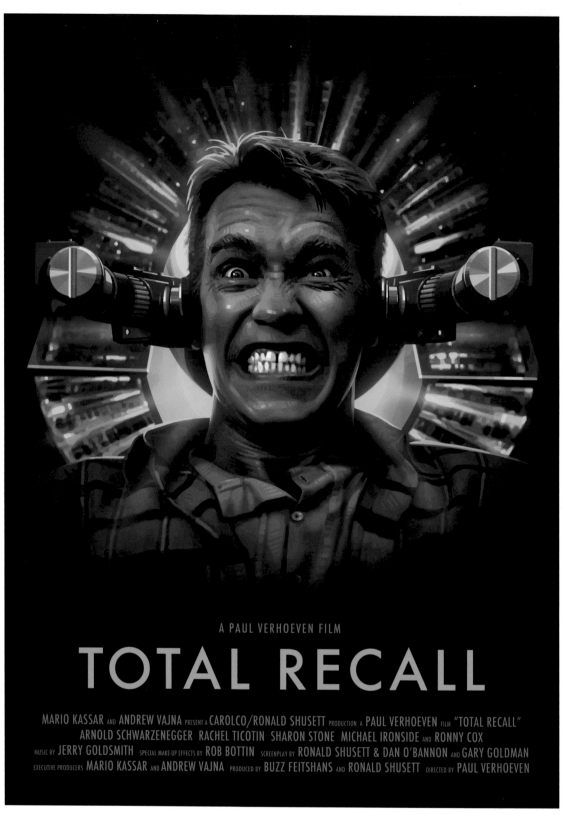

A PAUL VERHOEVEN FILM

TOTAL RECALL

MARIO KASSAR AND ANDREW VAJNA PRESENT A CAROLCO/RONALD SHUSETT PRODUCTION A PAUL VERHOEVEN FILM "TOTAL RECALL"
ARNOLD SCHWARZENEGGER RACHEL TICOTIN SHARON STONE MICHAEL IRONSIDE AND RONNY COX
MUSIC BY JERRY GOLDSMITH SPECIAL MAKE-UP EFFECTS BY ROB BOTTIN SCREENPLAY BY RONALD SHUSETT & DAN O'BANNON AND GARY GOLDMAN
EXECUTIVE PRODUCERS MARIO KASSAR AND ANDREW VAJNA PRODUCED BY BUZZ FEITSHANS AND RONALD SHUSETT DIRECTED BY PAUL VERHOEVEN

ALIAS	Candykiller
LOCATION	Dundee, Scotland / UK
SITE	Candykiller.com

BEHIND THE POSTERS: I was a huge fan of the original *Alien* [right], and while *Aliens* took a different approach with its "gung-ho marines in space" scenario, it is still a very good sequel. I was especially impressed with the Alien Queen design and decided to make her the subject for my poster design. I was similarly impressed with Paul Verhoeven's excursions into the science fiction genre, first with *RoboCop* and then *Total Recall*. Both films displayed a nice dry wit and amazing visual effects for the time. My *Total Recall* poster is intended to be the first in a three-part Arnie set, that will likely include *Terminator 2: Judgment Day* and *Predator*.

INFLUENCES: Artists—Jean (Moebius) Giraud, Drew Struzan, Ashley Wood, Chris Ware, Charles Burns, Robert Crumb, Harvey Kurtzman, Mort Drucker. Film directors—Ridley Scott, David Fincher, Guillermo del Toro, David Lynch. Art directors / designers—Vaughan Oliver, Neville Brody, Peter Saville.

FAVORITE FILM / GENRE: My favorite genre has to be science fiction, and my favorite film is *Blade Runner*. I went to see it three times in the cinema the week it was released (yes, I'm that old) and have probably watched it over 100 times over the years in various formats. It would be fair to say that I've always been a little obsessed with *Blade Runner* and no other movie has topped it since. The excellent documentary *Dangerous Days* that was included with the "final cut" version of *Blade Runner* on DVD and Blu-ray is also well worth checking out.

Brian Taylor

ALIAS	Candykiller
LOCATION	Dundee, Scotland / UK
SITE	Candykiller.com

TWENTIETH CENTURY-FOX PRESENTS

ALIENS

A BRANDYWINE PRODUCTION A JAMES CAMERON FILM "ALIENS" STARRING SIGOURNEY WEAVER
MUSIC BY JAMES HORNER ALIEN EFFECTS CREATED BY STAN WINSTON CERTAIN SPECIAL VISUAL EFFECTS CREATED BY THE L.A. EFFECTS GROUP, INC.
EXECUTIVE PRODUCERS GORDON CARROLL, DAVID GILER AND WALTER HILL BASED ON CHARACTERS CREATED BY DAN O'BANNON AND RONALD SHUSETT
STORY BY JAMES CAMERON AND DAVID GILER & WALTER HILL PRODUCED BY GALE ANNE HURD DIRECTED BY JAMES CAMERON

FIRST FILM: *Fantastic Voyage* was the first film that I remember going to see. The idea of a manned submarine, shrunk to microscopic size and injected into someone's bloodstream has stuck in my mind over the years. I'm sure that I must have seen other films before this, including the classic Disney features, but *Fantastic Voyage* is the first film that I remember sitting in the cinema and enjoying.

PREFERRED MEDIUM: A lot of my work is done digitally these days (Photoshop) but I still like to keep my hand involved, working in traditional painting and illustration once in a while. Everything that I do starts out as pencil and paper sketches, even if they will ultimately be produced on the computer.

CLIENTS: I don't generally do client work these days, preferring to create my own self-initiated projects including original paintings, prints, books, and posters. However, I just completed poster designs for two independent movies—the Australian science fiction thriller *Infini* and the British teen / family science fiction adventure *Robot Overlords*.

ADDITIONAL REMARKS: Having worked in illustration professionally for over thirty years now, movie poster design is a relatively new venture for me, but I am having a lot of fun working on them and plan to produce many more.

La Mala Educación
28 × 39 in (70 × 100 cm)

LOCATION Belgrade / Serbia
SITE Behance.net/marijabg

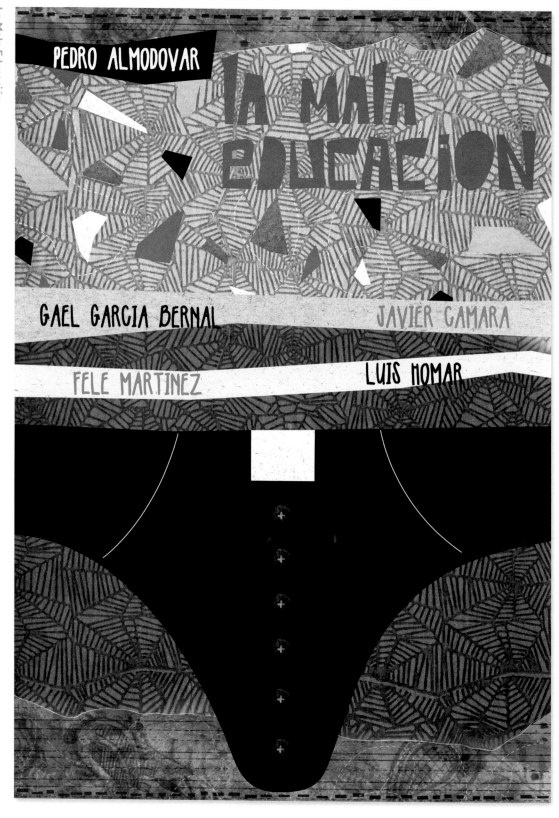

BEHIND THE POSTERS: I am a huge fan of Pedro Almodóvar. In my final year at the University of Applied Arts in Belgrade, we had to choose a project for our student exhibition. I decided to design a collection of posters inspired by Almodóvar's movies. I love how Almodóvar takes on strong stories that represent different groups of people, often with awkward life stories, making his films surreal yet breathtaking.

INFLUENCES: Stanley Kubrick, Emir Kusturica, Slobodan Šijan, and of course Pedro Almodóvar. I love all of their work and have watched some of their films so many times that I stopped counting.

FAVORITE FILM / GENRE: I enjoy a mix of black/European-style humor and drama. This is always a great combination. Favorite films include *Todo Sobre Mi Madre* and *La Mala Educación* (both by Almodóvar). Plus Emir Kusturica's *When Father Was Away on Business* and *Black Cat White Cat*, Slobodan Šijan's *Strangler vs. Strangler*, and many more from great Serbian directors.

Marija Marković

| LOCATION | Belgrade / Serbia |
| SITE | Behance.net/marijabg |

FIRST FILM: I cannot remember the first film that I ever watched, but two films that I fell in love with immediately were *Todo Sobre Mi Madre* and *Strangler vs. Strangler* (which many would say is not likeable, but in my opinion is a real rarity in cinematography).

ADDITIONAL REMARKS: I am excited that my work is going to be published in a book where people can see such a variety of images. It may sound like a cliché, but there are some films that can change your life and point of view. The poster is an extension of this idea, with the goal of captivating the viewer before even seeing the film.

BEHIND THE POSTERS: For the *True Romance* print, I really liked the cupid concept (a symbol of love), and how it portrays the title of the movie. Everything inside the cupid captures the violent spirit of the movie, while at the same time conveying the unique the love between Clarence and Alabama. I am particularly pleased with the typography on this one.

With *Escape from New York* my intention was to deliver a print that was less character-based, instead focusing on the film's atmosphere (while at the same time being true to the original poster artwork). Being a fan of the original and iconic poster, my print includes the post-apocalyptic streets of New York City, gang members, and the majestic Statue of Liberty (or what was left of it). Snake Plissken is all by himself: tired, hurt, on the run, and fighting against all odds.

RECENT PROJECTS: I have several screenprints that haven't been announced yet, and I have a feeling some of them will really excite fans. Recently I had the pleasure of working on an authorized poster (for Grey Matter Art and Studio Canal) that was based on one of my favorite David Lynch films, *Mulholland Drive.* I was also involved in a collaborative project between my brother Krzysztof and I, delivering two digital prints for Bottleneck Gallery's show "Turtles In Time," an official TMNT art show celebrating thirty years of "Turtle Power."

I also enjoyed working on cover illustration for Tobe Hooper's *The Texas Chainsaw Massacre Part 2*, which was part of a DVD / Blu-ray cover project run by Skuzzles, 20th Century Fox, and MGM Studio. Last but not least, I'm very pleased with a promotional poster that I created for a role-playing game, *The Witcher 3: Wild Hunt*, which I made for CD Projekt RED. This game is going to be epic.

Grzegorz Domaradzki

ALIAS	Gabz
LOCATION	Poznań / Poland
SITE	Iamgabz.com

1997.

New York City
is a walled maximum
security prison.

Breaking out
is impossible.

Breaking in
is insane.

John Carpenter's
ESCAPE FROM NEW YORK

JOHN CARPENTER'S "ESCAPE FROM NEW YORK" A DEBRA HILL PRODUCTION KURT RUSSELL · LEE VAN CLEEF · ERNEST BORGNINE
DONALD PLEASENCE · ISAAC HAYES · HARRY DEAN STANTON as "BRAIN" and ADRIENNE BARBEAU as "MAGGIE"
DIRECTOR OF PHOTOGRAPHY DEAN CUNDEY PRODUCTION DESIGNER JOE ALVES WRITTEN BY JOHN CARPENTER & NICK CASTLE PRODUCED BY LARRY FRANCO & DEBRA HILL DIRECTED BY JOHN CARPENTER

PINCH ME MOMENT: It's hard to select one favorite experience. I have been lucky in that most of my screenprints have received a nice amount of coverage online, with blog posts and interviews.

I recently was involved in an interesting project with a Polish company, Platige Image. They asked that I design a poster for what seemed to be a science fiction movie titled *Ambition*. However, in the end it was actually part of the promotion of an actual European Space Agency initiative called "The Rosetta Mission." I was very pleased with the final result.

IS THE FILM INDUSTRY COMING ALONG? Back in the days, when posters were mainly illustrated or painted, the viewer could truly imagine what movie they were about to experience. Now it's far too obvious, still. Being a huge fan of the Polish poster school, and many posters from that era, I wish that studios and filmmakers would start paying more attention to the quality of their designs. Film posters are not simply an advertisement of the film, but rather much more.

CLIENTS: Studio Canal, Paramount, Morgan Creek, MGM, 20th Century Fox, Warner Bros., Legendary Pictures, Hasbro, Nike, Reebok, 55DSL, Ubisoft, CD Projekt RED, and more.

ADDITIONAL REMARKS: Stay creative and inspired!

Erica Williams

The Secret of NIMH
18 × 24 in (46 × 61 cm)

LOCATION Minneapolis, Minnesota / US

SITE Ericawilliamsillustration.com

BEHIND THE POSTERS: Both were requests. Bottleneck Gallery inquired about creating *The Wonderful Wizard of Oz* poster, and Odd City Entertainment asked me to create *The Secret of NIMH*. I was really excited to work on *The Secret of NIMH* in particular because it was one of the movies that I grew up on.

INFLUENCES: Hayao Miyazaki has been a huge influence on me since I can remember. CLAMP, a group of all-female manga artists, is another one that I adore. More traditional artists would have to include Albrecht Durer, Arthur Rackham, Warwick Goble, Mucha, Saturnino Herran, and John Singer Sargent. A couple of the directors I really love are Danny Boyle and Lars von Trier.

FAVORITE FILM / GENRE: I am a huge fan of dystopian films. I can't really pick a favorite but a couple of my favorite films are *Antichrist*, *Blade Runner*, and pretty much anything Miyazaki has done. Miyazaki is a genre right? He totally deserves his own genre.

FIRST FILM: Oh man, umm. *Antichrist*. I think everything about it was perfect. *Blade Runner* is a close second though. Both of them are insanely beautiful and have perfect cinematography. Both of them also have a lot of lore in them and that's always really important to me.

The Wonderful Wizard of Oz
18 × 24 in (46 × 61 cm)

Erica Williams

LOCATION Minneapolis, Minnesota / US

SITE Ericawilliamsillustration.com

PREFERRED MEDIUM: Ink. I like working with gouache as well, but am most attached to ink. Something about the permanence of ink and working in a traditional way really helps you hone your craft. I also really love that working traditionally leaves you with a physical original.

CLIENTS: The Black Keys, Surly Brewing, Ray LaMontagne, Baroness, QBP, and The Head and The Heart are a few.

ADDITIONAL REMARKS: You can never go wrong with waffles.

The Fly
24 × 36 in (61 × 91 cm)

BEHIND THE POSTERS: Some of my posters are commissioned by outside sources and the rest are demanded by a team of mischievous meerkats that live under my bed.

INFLUENCES: I am equally influenced by a crippling fear of failure and an overwhelming desire to stay in bed for as long as humanly possible.

FAVORITE FILM / GENRE: According to Netflix, my favorite genre is "romance driven suspense sci-fi coms," so, *Gilmore Girls*.

FIRST FILM: I don't remember. But I do remember seeing *Raiders of the Lost Ark* when it came out and relentlessly bugging my Mom to buy me a whip for months after. She never caved on that one.

ALIAS NoSupervision

LOCATION Richmond, Virginia / US

SITE Nosupervision.tumblr.com

The Girl with the Dragon Tattoo
24 × 36 in (61 × 91 cm)

THE GIRL WITH THE DRAGON TATTOO   DANIEL CRAIG   ROONEY MARA

PREFERRED MEDIUM: Zoltar.
CLIENTS: Everyone from Pepsi and Criterion to friends who need wedding invitations.

ADDITIONAL REMARKS: Someone buy me a whip.

Dave Perillo

National Lampoon's Vacation
(actual title = *Walley World*)
18 × 24 in (46 × 61 cm)

LOCATION Philadelphia, Pennsylvania / US

SITE Montygog.blogspot.com

BEHIND THE POSTERS: Both pieces were created for a two-man show I had with artist Tom Whalen at Gallery 1988 in August 2012. The theme was '80s movies/television shows reimagined as vintage travel posters.

RECENT PROJECTS: Most of the projects I work on are hush-hush until the film gets released, but in August 2014, I had my first solo exhibition at Gallery 1988. It was a blast. I also had the opportunity to design a few Vinylmations for Disney and hope to do more in the future.

PINCH ME MOMENT: Recently I had the opportunity to create posters for the band The Aquabats. I had been a fan for years and was able to meet and hang out with the guys. When they came around to Philly to play a show, MC Bat Commander gave me a shout out on stage for the poster art.

TRAVELING TO FANTASIA? NOTHING BEATS...

FALKOR AIR

THE LUCKIEST WAY TO FLY!

▼ Dave Perillo

LOCATION Philadelphia, Pennsylvania / US

SITE Montygog.blogspot.com

The Neverending Story
(actual title = *Falkor Air*)
18 × 24 in (46 × 61 cm)

IS THE FILM INDUSTRY COMING ALONG? I think that the film industry is finally starting to take note of these original artistic interpretations of movies. You will definitely be seeing the industry using more and more of them in their marketing and promotions.

CLIENTS: Disney, Mondo, Target, Acme Archives, Gallery 1988, Spoke Art Gallery, Acid Free Gallery, Dark Hall Mansion.

The Shining
24 × 36 in (61 × 91 cm)

BEHIND THE POSTERS: I am in the midst of covering Stanley Kubrick's entire body of work (a long-term project). *The Shining* and *A Clockwork Orange* are two of the first pieces.
INFLUENCES: I am aiming for the directness of a Tadanori Yokoo style frontal assault (with the figure treatment of Frank Quitely).

FAVORITE FILM / GENRE: Realistic, drama-based science fiction.

A Clockwork Orange
24 × 36 in (61 × 91 cm)

FIRST FILM: *Tarzan* (the Johnny Weissmuller version).
PREFERRED MEDIUM: Digital.

CLIENTS: These particular posters were private commissions. Other clients include Universal Pictures, IFC, Lucas Films, *Time*, *The New Yorker*, *The New York Times*, *Rolling Stone*, MTV, Saatchi & Saatchi, BBDo, Nike, *GQ*, *Esquire*, Warner Bros., DC, Marvel, Scholastic, Random House, Penguin, Microsoft, *Playboy*, Fantagraphics, *The Progressive*, *Entertainment Weekly*, American Red Cross, and *Newsweek*.

Back to the Future
28 × 36 in (70 × 91 cm)

LOCATION Llandudno, Wales / UK

SITE Andyfairhurstart.com

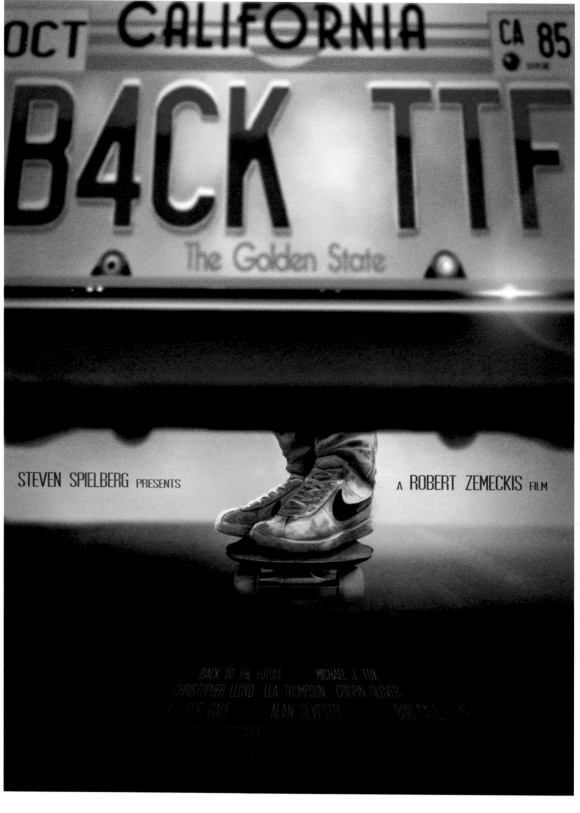

STEVEN SPIELBERG PRESENTS   A ROBERT ZEMECKIS FILM

BACK TO THE FUTURE   MICHAEL J FOX
CHRISTOPHER LLOYD   LEA THOMPSON   CRISPIN GLOVER
BOB GALE   ALAN SILVESTRI   BOB GALE

BEHIND THE POSTERS: If *Star Wars* was the film that got me into art as a young kid, then *Back to the Future* was the film that defined me as a young teen. I watched it every weekend for six weeks when it came out, and it has stayed with me ever since. I wanted to be Marty.

INFLUENCES: My Influences are pretty much the same as a lot of artists, Spielberg, *Star Wars*, and practically half the films of the '70s and '80s. I get a lot of inspiration from music, too.

FAVORITE FILM / GENRE: I have too many to mention, but *The Empire Strikes Back, Mad Max 2, The Breakfast Club, Alien,* and *Stand By Me* are always high on my list. My favorite genres are a toss-up between sci-fi and action-adventure. I love most genres but come back to these two more often than not.

FIRST FILM: The first film I remember as a kid at the cinema was *The Rescuers*, which I saw just before *Star Wars*.
PREFERRED MEDIUM: Digital painting. I use Photoshop CS6.
CLIENTS: BBC, Big Chief Studios, Hartswood Films.

ADDITIONAL REMARKS: Since discovering alternative film posters I have found a plethora of amazing artists, especially through the Poster Posse, who have opened my eyes to other techniques. My love for films has always been huge. I only wish that I had discovered alternative movie posters years ago.

Rocky IV
(actual title = *Constructivist Pugilist Manifest No. 4*)
18 × 24 in (46 × 61 cm)

LOCATION New York, New York / US

SITE Anthonypetrie.com

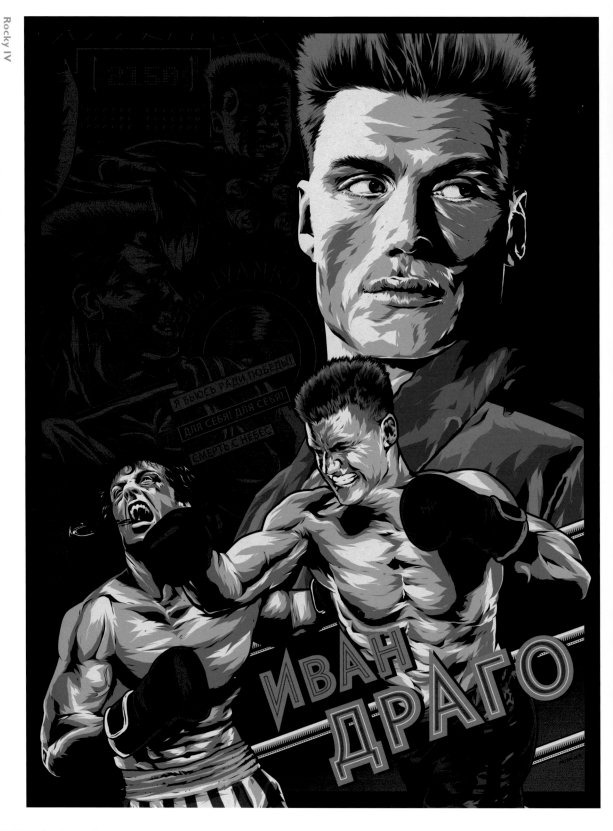

BEHIND THE POSTERS: The *Rocky IV*-inspired print was part of Gallery 1988's "Crazy 4 Cult" show that celebrated villains from movies. Since it's one of my favorite movies, I really wanted to recreate the "training montage" scene for Drago, but through a Russian constructivist lens. The *Ghostbusters* poster was part of the 30th anniversary art show with Sony. It was one of the few posters in the show that received actor likeness approval.

RECENT PROJECTS: I am finishing up a solo show at Gallery 1988. The past year has been busy and exciting with projects such as editorial illustrations for *WWE Magazine*, a gig poster for Fall Out Boy and Paramore, and many official gallery shows (for Edgar Wright, Joss

Whedon, *Adventure Time*, etc.). I have some Sony Blu-ray steel case special edition covers coming out soon, and I have been freelancing full-time for Nickelodeon on *Teenage Mutant Ninja Turtles*.

PINCH ME MOMENT: I did a signing for the Gallery 1988/Sony *Ghostbusters* thirtieth anniversary show at San Diego Comic Con 2014, and there was a poster fan and artist meet-and-greet. In both instances, it was great to chat and have some drinks with people who are passionate about my work and the community as a whole. At San Diego Comic Con '13 I similarly did a signing with the cast and crew of *Sharknado* with official posters that I created for the SyFy network. I heard that Sylvester Stallone bought one of my Ivan Drago prints from Gallery 1988, and that Arsenio Hall picked up one of my *Coming to America* posters.

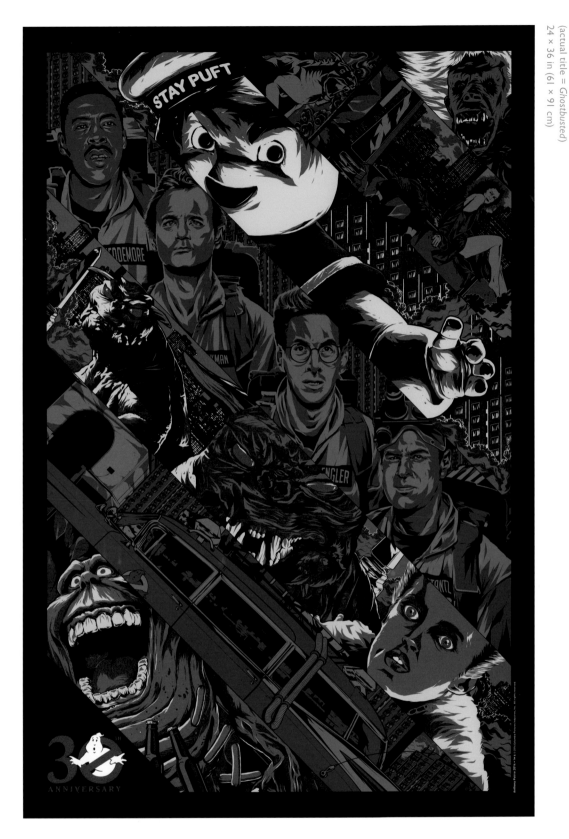

Ghostbusters
(actual title = Ghostbusted)
24 × 36 in (61 × 91 cm)

Anthony Petrie

LOCATION New York, New York / US

SITE Anthonypetrie.com

IS THE FILM INDUSTRY COMING ALONG? In terms of key art created for movies, there has definitely been a noticeable infusion of "alternative subculture" art concepts and aesthetics. Production companies and design firms look to the subgenre of alternative movie posters for inspiration in mainstream marketing projects. Additionally, the more popular a traditional artist gets, the more mainstream work opportunities they will receive. I think that overall the modern poster movement serves as a trendsetter for all printed material in the graphic design, illustration, and marketing worlds.

CLIENTS: Marvel, Nickelodeon, Adidas, Reebok, CrossFit, UFC, Spartan Race, Sony, Paramount, Cartoon Network, The Academy, Bad Robot, SyFy, CBS, NBC, FOX, AMC, NFL, MLB, NHL.

ADDITIONAL REMARKS: You can also follow my work at zombiebacons.tumblr.com, behance.net/anthonypetrie, @zombiebacons on Twitter and Instagram.

Oli Riches

Captain America: The Winter Soldier
16 × 24 in (41 × 61 cm)

LOCATION Oslo / Norway (originally from England)

SITE Oliriches.com

MARVEL STUDIOS
presents

CAPTAIN AMERICA
THE WINTER SOLDIER

BEHIND THE POSTERS: I've always been a fan of superheroes, so it seemed like a natural choice to take on two films that I was really passionate about. *Captain America* was more about trying to make an iconic poster, and I liked the idea of using negative space in the form of a star to realize Captain America's symbol. With *Man of Steel*, I was inspired by the line "What if a child dreamed of becoming something other than what society had intended? What if a child aspired to something greater?" To capture the concept that Clark would grow up to be the greatest hero, I wanted to focus the artwork on him as an innocent boy playing on his farm, with a secondary and subtle detail in the clouds of Superman flying.

INFLUENCES: My main influences are the films and characters themselves. Simply watching trailers usually sparks off ideas. Ridley Scott in particular was a major influence, as it was *Gladiator* that led me to study animation and embark on a creative career. In regard to movie posters, Drew Struzan and Saul Bass are great inspirations, as are the likes of Olly Moss and Matt Taylor. I also love children's book illustrators like Quentin Blake.

MAN OF STEEL

WARNER BROS. PICTURES PRESENTS
IN ASSOCIATION WITH LEGENDARY PICTURES A SYNCOPY PRODUCTION A ZACK SNYDER FILM "MAN OF STEEL" HENRY CAVILL AMY ADAMS MICHAEL SHANNON KEVIN COSTNER DIANE LANE
LAURENCE FISHBURNE ANTJE TRAUE AYELET ZURER AND RUSSELL CROWE   JAMES ACHESON MICHAEL WILKINSON   HANS ZIMMER   DAVID BRENNER
ALEX MCDOWELL   AMIR MOKRI   JERRY SIEGEL & JOE SHUSTER   DC ENTERTAINMENT   THOMAS TULL CLOYD PHILLIPS JON PETERS
DAVID S. GOYER & CHRISTOPHER NOLAN   DAVID S. GOYER   CHARLES ROVEN CHRISTOPHER NOLAN EMMA THOMAS DEBORAH SNYDER   ZACK SNYDER

FAVORITE FILM / GENRE: It's tough to pick a favorite, so here are five: *Gladiator, Iron Giant, Predator, Raiders of the Lost Ark*, and *The Dark Knight*.
FIRST FILM: I remember crying as a four-year-old at the cinema watching *The Land Before Time*, so I guess that was it. Plus I had the *The Jungle Book, Robin Hood*, and *The Sword in the Stone* playing constantly.

PREFERRED MEDIUM: I enjoy traditional drawing as well as digital/ vector work.

Darin Shock

A Christmas Story
18 × 24 in (46 × 61 cm)

LOCATION Cincinnati, Kentucky / US

SITE Stateofshockstudios.com

BEHIND THE POSTERS: *A Christmas Story* is not only the ultimate Christmas classic, I'm prepared to declare it one of my favorite films of all time. It's a simple tale with many rich layers and comedic hard truths about childhood. Although I didn't grow up in the time period, it paints such a vivid picture that it somehow seems familiar. I'm also fascinated with the buildup to Christmas. Simply put, no film is capable of making me feel like a kid more than *A Christmas Story*, and I like feeling like a kid . . . there's no mortgage or mouth sores. These elements, plus the fact that I've never seen an art print for this film = yes, I'll do a poster for *that*! Also, I'm a huge, huge fan of the absurd genius of *Monty Python and the Holy Grail*. It is, in my opinion, Python at their best. They changed the game and this was their masterpiece. It was an honor to have to watch it

no less than fifteen times while doing research and designing. This film never gets old. I'm also proud to say that it's probably my girlfriend's favorite film, which is sexy as hell!

INFLUENCES: This could go on and on, so I'll just list the first ten that come to mind: R. Crumb, Frank Zappa, Tim Burton, Drew Struzan, John K, Louis CK, Martin Ansin, Rick Phelps, Wes Anderson, Wayne White, Kevin Dart, Gerardo, Dave Chappelle, Jonathan Edwards, Michael Cho, and Luke from The Bushwhackers.

FAVORITE FILM / GENRE: Burton's *Batman*. I was ten when it came out and it had a major impact on my life. I currently own Batman

LOCATION Cincinnati, Kentucky / US

SITE Stateofshockstudios.com

underwear and attribute it directly to that film. Simply put, no other movie has influenced my purchasing of underwear as an adult. That's partly because I've never seen *Shawshank Redemption* underwear, but still.

FIRST FILM: I have a lot of early memories of movies but cannot really put them in order. I'll go with *E.T.* or *9 1/2 Weeks.*

PREFERRED MEDIUM: Miss Cleo.

ADDITIONAL REMARKS: I believe that it was twentieth-century philosopher Ice Cube who once said "Life ain't nothin' but bitches and money." It's been my motto since the fifth grade and it still holds true to this day. Kinda.

Keith Ten Eyck

It
11 × 17 in (28 × 43 cm)

ALIAS	Keithist
LOCATION	Cleveland, Ohio / US
SITE	Dribbble.com/keithist

BEHIND THE POSTERS: I was thinking of influential movies that stood out to me as a child (and universally to other people as well). Stephen King had such a huge following for his books and films in the '80s. Plus, to be honest, I was vending at an event, and I wanted to make sure I had some big sellers.

INFLUENCES: Saul Bass, Robert Béreny, Paul Rand, Michael Haneke, Sion Soto, Gustave Doré, Aaron Horkey, Steven Shainberg, Paolo Sorrentino, any/every Polish artist—ever.

FAVORITE FILM / GENRE: Industry-specific period pieces, transgressive dramas, and character studies. I can't name just one, but *Phase IV* (1974), *Tras el Cristal*, *The President's Last Bang*, *The Thing*, *Fist of Legend*, *Le Salaire de la Peur*, *Akira*.

지금, 공포의 새 이름이있다.

STEPHEN KING
CUJO
쿠죠

▼

Keith Ten Eyck

ALIAS   Keithist
LOCATION   Cleveland, Ohio / US
SITE   Dribbble.com/keithist

FIRST FILM: Damn. Wow . . . *Total Recall, Breaker Breaker, Enter the Dragon, Bambi, Cinderella.*
PREFERRED MEDIUM: Digital illustration.

ADDITIONAL REMARKS: Here are the top three movies that I have seen the most but haven't watched in ten to twenty years: 1) *Wayne's World*, 2) *From Dusk till Dawn*, 3) *Empire Records*. Also, I don't like *Star Wars* . . . I grew up on *Kung Fu* films.

BEHIND THE POSTERS: A lot of my illustration is heavy with pop culture references, much of which is horror related. I equate that to growing up watching the old Universal Monsters classics on weekend afternoons, plus a passion for loud/heavy rock music (they seem to go hand-in-hand). Between concert and movie posters, I've gravitated toward horror as a recurring subject to depict for both. It's interesting how these two very different movie pieces tie together in my portfolio.

The *Halloween II* poster is from 2009 and was initially created for a fan art contest judged by Rob Zombie himself. The poster did not win the contest, but it did lead to bigger things. A year later I was asked to do an event poster for a midnight screening of *Pumpkinhead*, and the host of the screening was also the coordinator for the Rob Zombie contest. My *Halloween*

II poster is still fairly easy to find on Rob Zombie's webSite and Facebook fan page, and I have since been able to personally give prints to Scout Taylor Compton and Tyler Mane from the film, as well as to Mr. Zombie himself. *Pumpkinhead* was available for purchase in limited supply at the screening at New Beverly Cinema in Los Angeles, for whom I have since created a few more midnight movie posters.

INFLUENCES: When it comes to illustrated movie posters, you can't get better than Mr. Drew Struzan. And there are a few directors who I absolutely love: Guillermo del Toro, Tim Burton, Jim Henson, John Carpenter . . . I could go on. Doing my own versions of film posters has been a great way to feel like a part of the movies I love. It has also pushed my art in front of a few of my favorite directors, including del Toro and Carpenter.

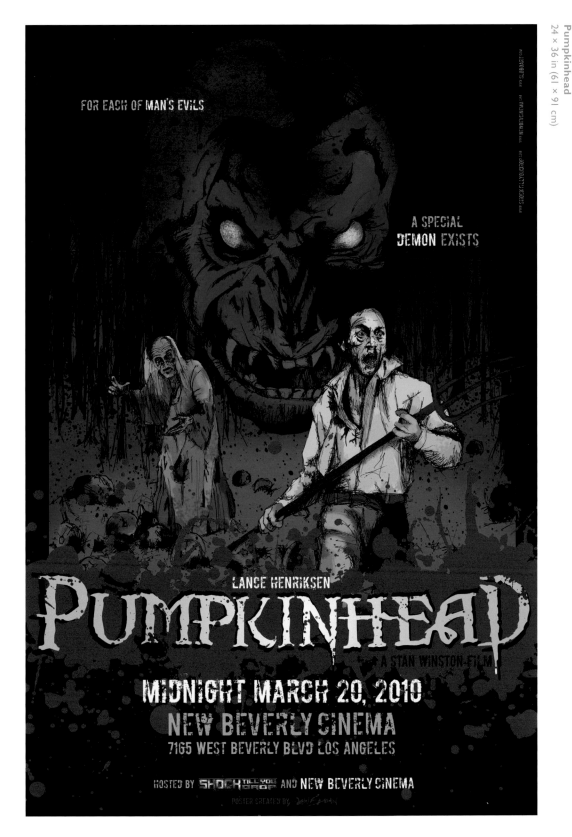

FOR EACH OF MAN'S EVILS

A SPECIAL
DEMON EXISTS

LANCE HENRIKSEN

PUMPKINHEAD

A STAN WINSTON FILM

MIDNIGHT MARCH 20, 2010

NEW BEVERLY CINEMA

7165 WEST BEVERLY BLVD LOS ANGELES

HOSTED BY SHOCK TILL YOU DROP AND NEW BEVERLY CINEMA

POSTER CREATED BY

Pumpkinhead
24 × 36 in (61 × 91 cm)

FAVORITE FILM / GENRE: Tie. *Return of the Jedi / Legend*. Read from that what you will. I think this also means that fantasy would be my favorite genre, but there's no denying that I love horror.

FIRST FILM: Apparently I saw *E.T.* at a drive-in when I was only two. I remember gravitating toward movies like *Star Wars*, *Back to the Future*, and *Labyrinth*—the really imaginative stuff.

PREFERRED MEDIUM: I start with ballpoint pen every time. That line drawing gets digitally scanned, and then I color digitally. Sometimes I add some vector art in the design or splash some ink around with a paint brush, toothbrush, etc. The digital element has evolved as my graphic design has improved, but it always starts with that ballpoint pen illustration.

CLIENTS: So far I have created posters for New Beverly Cinema, Cleveland Cinemas, ScreamFest L.A., and several private clients. I have been able to spin that into additional art for events like Eerie Horror Film Fest, Walker Stalker Con, and AMC television. I also like to create the occasional piece for group shows at galleries when the subject grabs me.

ALIAS Uncle Gertrude

LOCATION Knoxville, Tennessee / US

SITE Etsy.com/shop/UncleGertrudes

Pink Flamingos
12 × 18 in (30 × 46 cm)

BEHIND THE POSTERS: *Pink Flamingos* is an old favorite. I discovered Divine and John Waters in college. A group of my friends from the art department and I would unwind in the dorm watching John Waters' movies. I fell in love with Divine! The image of her in that iconic dress waving a gun was forever etched in my brain.

For *Grey Gardens*, it wasn't until I watched the movie with Drew Barrymore and Jessica Lange that I became fascinated by Big and Little Edie. I immediately ordered the documentary. I fell head over heels in love with Little Edie the first time I watched. From her revolutionary fashion to her S-T-A-U-N-C-H character, she was a star needing to shine.

INFLUENCES: My influences are vast. As a graphic designer, I am used to pleasing clients with an array of styles. But doing these posters has been wonderful to find my own voice. I get to be my own client, although I think I am my most difficult client. There are lots of subjects, films, music, television shows, and personalities that excite me, and my posters develop from these influences.

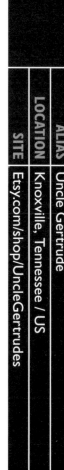

Grey Gardens
12 × 18 in (30 × 46 cm)

MEET JACKIE-O'S SCANDALOUS RELATIVES
THE RICHES TO RAGS STORY OF EDITH BOUVIER BEALE AND HER DAUGHTER, "LITTLE EDIE" BEALE

This is the best thing to wear for the day, you understand, because I don't like women in skirts, and the best thing is to wear pantyhose or some pants under a short skirt I think, then you have the pants under the skirt, and then you pull the stockings up over the pants underneath the skirt and you can always take off the skirt and you it as a cape! I think this is the best costume for the day! I have to think these things up, you know....mother wanted me to come out in a kimono so we had quite a fight.

©1975

GREY GARDENS

A DOCUMENTARY FILM BY ALBERT AND DAVID MAYSLES

FAVORITE FILM / GENRE: My love of films varies. I love horror and campy movies.
FIRST FILM: *The Shining* was one of the first that I remember seeing. The Grady twins scared the hell out of me. Last year, I was lucky enough to get the twins to autograph a poster that I did of *The Shining* featuring them.
PREFERRED MEDIUM: My medium of choice is to create digitally, and I love typography. Design is not just a job that pays the mortgage, it's what I love to do.

CLIENTS: I used to work for a television production company and created graphics for various networks. But my favorite experience was when ABC's *Nashville* called to request one of my posters to use on set.
ADDITIONAL REMARKS: I would like to thank my partner, Steve Polyak. Without his encouragement and support, I would have never started doing these posters.

The Incredibles
20 × 30 in (50 × 76 cm)

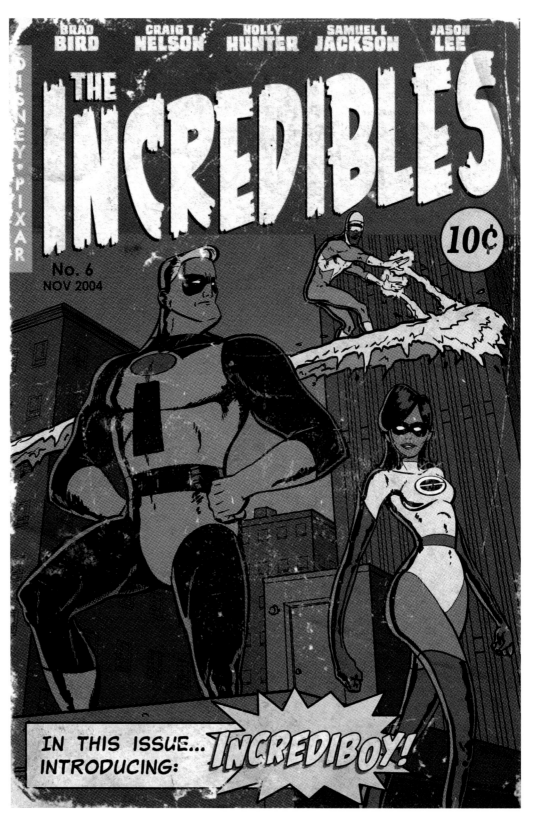

LOCATION Orlando, Florida / US
SITE Timothyandersonart.com

BEHIND THE POSTERS: *The Incredibles* poster was for a Hero Complex Gallery show, "The Oscars," and any films that had won an Academy Award was fair game. I have always been a huge fan of Pixar and Brad Bird, so I jumped at the chance to have a go with one of my favorite films. An old comic book cover was the obvious choice for a superhero movie, and because so much of the movie is about Mr. Incredible yearning for the "glory days," I thought that a Silver Age of Comics style was appropriate.

The Matrix poster was an homage to old pulp science fiction magazines. I had the idea to give modern sci-fi classics a retro twist by depicting them as if they'd been published in the '60s as cheap novels and magazines. Those books were inexpensively produced and relied heavily on eye-catching images

and intriguing taglines, so my objective was to incorporate those elements. In fact, the tagline I went with, "They're killing machines designed for one thing: Search and Destroy," has probably been the biggest magnet for snarky Internet comments. "Um, isn't that two things?" they smugly ask, clearly unaware that it's a line directly from the movie, which is kind of the joke. Having said that, I suppose *I'm* the snarky one now.

INFLUENCES: I try to steal a tiny bit from a lot of different people in an effort to pass off the theft as a personal style, which is probably why my style is constantly shifting. I admire the brilliant simplicity of Tom Whalen's designs, while on the other end of the spectrum, I love getting lost in the detailed drawings of Tyler Stout, Joshua Budich, and Chris Weston. There's so much great stuff out there, and I'm constantly discovering new artists who inspire me.

The Matrix
24 × 36 in (61 × 91 cm)

MORPHEUS BOOKS
75¢

THE MATRIX

They're killing machines designed for one thing: SEARCH AND DESTROY!

LOCATION Orlando, Florida / US

SITE Timothyandersonart.com

FAVORITE FILM / GENRE: As one could probably gather from my portfolio, my favorite genre is science fiction, and my favorite film is the classic Star Wars trilogy ("Um, isn't that three films?" To which I say, "Yes, but shut up.")

FIRST FILM: The first film I ever saw was *Raiders of the Lost Ark*. I was a little less than three months old and my parents brought me to the theater with them in whatever passed for a baby carrier back then (perhaps an old shoe box or something). While I clearly don't remember that experience, I've been a life-long *Indiana Jones* fanboy, and those three films are in my all-time top ten ("Um, weren't there four?"—"Shut up.").

PREFERRED MEDIUM: While most of my pieces begin as rough pencil or pen drawings in a sketchbook, I take everything into the computer fairly early in the process and design/paint them digitally. The computer is much cleaner to work on than traditional media (a significant fact especially now that I have three young sons running around the house) and takes up far less space. Many of my pieces are ultimately screen printed, though, so they eventually make their way back to a traditional medium.

CLIENTS: As far as my posters and illustrations, I've worked with Acme Archives, Lollapalooza, Rooster Teeth, and a handful of others. I've also worked as Concept Designer for various film and video game studios. I'm currently an attraction designer for Universal Studios, and I create my posters in the evenings and on weekends.

Danger Diabolik
27 × 40 in (69 × 102 cm)

LOCATION London / UK

SITE Jamesgilleard.com

BEHIND THE POSTERS: These were created for two different gallery shows, *The Man with the Golden Gun* [right] for a Hero Complex's "Weapon of Choice" show, and *Danger Diabolik* for Planet Pulp's "Red" gallery exhibit. I had always wanted to create a poster for *Danger Diabolik*, and the Bond image used here was a year-old sketch that I thought fit the theme perfectly.

RECENT PROJECTS: I have been working on numerous projects, including educational and healthcare animations, kids' apps, picture books, and editorial images. I have not (yet) created any official Blu-ray covers or theatrical posters, although this would be great.

PINCH ME MOMENT: A recent image that I created for the eighty-fifth anniversary of *Popeye* exhibition went down well. However, a poster I made for *The Life Aquatic* pretty much started my illustration career and got the ball rolling!

IS THE FILM INDUSTRY COMING ALONG? From what I have seen it might be getting a bit better, with individual illustrators producing covers for Blu-rays again. I hope this continues.
CLIENTS: Disney, Paul McCartney, BT, Penguin, Vodaphone, Alere, BBC, ITV, MC Saatchi.

Clark Orr

Willy Wonka & the Chocolate Factory
(actual title = *Lick-Able Wallpaper* / contains scented ink)
18 × 24 in (46 × 61 cm)

DESIGN FIRM Clark Orr Design Co.

LOCATION DeLand, Florida / US

SITE Clarkorr.com

BEHIND THE POSTERS: *Lick-Able Wallpaper.* I came up with the idea to do a *Willy Wonka*-themed poster, and my friend and fellow illustrator Dave Quiggle suggested doing lickable wallpaper (from the well-known scene). A big theme in my work is interactivity and making each piece look like it has a place in the world. So I wanted the poster to look like wallpaper, as if lickable wallpaper actually existed. I also thought it would be a nice touch to have it printed using scented ink, so my print shop mixed fruit-scented oils with the ink.

Stay Puft. I have always been drawn to vintage advertisements from the '50s and '60s, and thought that it would be fun to create a vintage ad for Stay Puft® Marshmallows, subtly incorporating the *Ghostbusters*. Since I love interaction with my artwork, I included glow-in-the-dark elements in the negative space. When you hit the lights, proton packs shoot streams at Stay Puft (and I was careful not to cross the streams). I also thought it'd be fun to sneak in a glow-in-the-dark Slimer, having him eat marshmallows that he stole from the advertisement's illustration.

Ghostbusters
(actual title = *Stay Puft* / contains glow-in-the-dark ink)
18 × 24 in (46 × 61 cm)

DESIGN FIRM Clark Orr Design Co.
LOCATION DeLand, Florida / US
SITE Clarkorr.com

INFLUENCES: Stanley Kubrick, Alfred Hitchcock, Charley Harper, Saul Bass, Aesthetic Apparatus, Ed Roth, Sailor Jerry, Art Chantry, Dave Quiggle, Invisible Creature, Shepard Fairey, and a bunch of artists that are profiled in this book.
FAVORITE FILM / GENRE: *The Goonies* is my favorite movie, although I am always down for a good documentary.
FIRST FILM: The first movie I remember seeing in the theater was *The Land Before Time*. I would have been four years old.

PREFERRED MEDIUM: Digital illustration, silkscreen.
CLIENTS: Most people associate me with my decade-long career as head designer at Johnny Cupcakes. I have also done a lot of other work for various clients, both high and low profile.
ADDITIONAL REMARKS: Draw skulls.

The Umbrellas of Cherbourg
16 × 24 in (41 × 61 cm)

DESIGN FIRM Sam's Myth
LOCATION Nashville, Tennessee / US
SITE Samsmyth.blogspot.com

BEHIND THE POSTERS: The design for *The Umbrellas of Cherbourg* was one of a few images that I was hired to produce for Janus Films. It was created for the theatrical restoration of Jacques Demy's film. When Janus went in a different direction for the poster, I repurposed the design for the Belcourt Theatre in Nashville, TN. The *Vertigo* print was commissioned by The Castro Theatre (San Francisco, CA) and Spoke Art Gallery for a special 70mm presentation of the film in honor of The Castro Theatre's anniversary.

INFLUENCES: The masters of Cuban, Czech, and Polish poster art, Hans Hillmann, Saul Bass, Tadanori Yokoo, Jaroslav Sura, Ed Emberley, Dick Bruna, Paul Rand, Chris Van Allsburg, Tove Jansson, 100% Orange, Alain Grée, Alvin Lustig, Helen Borten, Penguin, Nobrow, Push Pin, Mike Davis, Jay Shaw, We Buy Your Kids, Blexbolex, Jon Klassen, Robert Hunter, and too many other designers, artists, musicians, writers, and thinkers to mention.

DESIGN FIRM Sam's Myth
LOCATION Nashville, Tennessee / US
SITE Samsmyth.blogspot.com

SPOKE ART & THE CASTRO THEATRE PROUDLY PRESENT

ALFRED HITCHCOCK'S

VERTIGO

PRESENTED IN 70mm

AUGUST 31 - SEPTEMBER 3 2012
THE CASTRO THEATRE
429 CASTRO ST.
SAN FRANCISCO

CASTROTHEATRE.COM · SPOKE-ART.COM

FAVORITE FILM / GENRE: *2001: A Space Odyssey*, tied with *My Neighbor Totoro*, with *Koyaanisqatsi* close behind. I particularly enjoy foreign cinema, animation, and obscure '80s fantasy films with ambient soundtracks.
FIRST FILM: *The Little Prince*, directed by Stanley Donen, which was the feature-length musical adaptation of the 1943 novella by Antoine de Saint-Exupéry.
PREFERRED MEDIUM: Drawing and cutouts, finished in Photoshop.

CLIENTS: Janus Films, The Criterion Collection, A24, IFC Films, Oscilloscope Laboratories, Cinedigm, Zeitgeist Films, Independent Cinema Office, Amplify, Death Waltz Records, Merge Records, Third Man Records, The Dissolve, The Nashville Symphony, *Nashville Scene*, Belcourt Theatre.
ADDITIONAL REMARKS: "The ball I threw while playing in the park has not yet touched the ground." —Dylan Thomas

Trigun
24 × 36 in (61 × 91 cm)

ALIAS	That Kid Who Draws
LOCATION	Austin, Texas / US
SITE	Thatkidwhodraws.com

BEHIND THE POSTERS: These were part of a personal project in which I re-imagined movie posters for my favorite Japanese animation films.

INFLUENCES: Yoshiyuki Sadamoto, Drew Struzan, Junji Ito, Alphonse Mucha.

ALIAS	That Kid Who Draws
LOCATION	Austin, Texas / US
SITE	Thatkidwhodraws.com

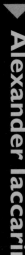

Ghost in the Shell
20 × 30 in (50 × 76 cm)

FAVORITE FILM / GENRE: Japanese animation, South Korean action/drama.
FIRST FILM: *Aladdin* is the earliest film I can remember watching and drawing characters from.

PREFERRED MEDIUM: Photoshop, Cintiq.
CLIENTS: AMC, Sony Entertainment, NBC Universal.

RoboCop
24 × 36 in (61 × 91 cm)

BEHIND THE POSTERS: The *RoboCop* prints were designed specifically for a themed exhibition at the Hero Complex Gallery titled "I am the Law / A Life of Crime." The original 1987 film release of *RoboCop* has long been a favorite, and I had been looking for an opportunity to do a print release. Needless to say, the exhibition offered me that chance, so I created an alternate print edition that showcased *RoboCop*'s transformation through the course of the film rather than just a more standard variant color offering.

INFLUENCES: My influences range from medium to medium, genre to genre. Some of my greatest influences from the past range from directors such as Steven Spielberg, Terry Gilliam, and Ridley Scott, to more recent directors such as Alfonso Cuarón and Guillermo del Toro (who are pushing visual storytelling in film to new heights). I have always been a huge fan of the beautifully illustrated works of Maxfield Parrish and N. C. Wyeth, but also find the photographic works of the Richard Avedon to be equally compelling and inspiring, particularly his collection "In the American West," a stunning series of portrait photography.

FAVORITE FILM / GENRE: I have to split my vote between two iconic films from the '80s by two iconic directors. Terry Gilliam's *Brazil* (1985), a love story laced with an incredible visual mix of both sci-fi and fantasy genres, set against the backdrop of a massive *1984* Orwellian-themed bureaucracy. It is Gilliam's masterpiece. My other equally endearing favorite film is Ridley Scott's *Blade Runner*. It is arguably the best overall sci-fi movie ever. The art direction alone is worth the watch, but when you mix in a dark, brooding detective/noir storyline topped with an equally iconic film score, you have the makings of a one-of-a-kind classic helmed by a master filmmaker.

FIRST FILM: *Pee-wee's Big Adventure*. I'd like to say *Return of the Jedi* but that'd be a lie (this was the second film I ever saw). Such is my legacy.
PREFERRED MEDIUM: Digital. There's something completely empowering about painting with light, albeit artificial light, but light nonetheless. I approach my digital work with somewhat traditional techniques, using minimal or no filters and a fairly limited brush set in Photoshop. I sketch and paint out every detail by hand as I would on paper or canvas. Traditional art forms will always hold a visual and tactile quality that digital will never be able to fully replicate, yet digital offers absolute control over practically every detail. I find this most gratifying.
ADDITIONAL REMARKS: Han shot first.

Pierre Kleinhouse

Reservoir Dogs
20 × 28 in (50 × 70 cm)

LOCATION Tel Aviv / Israel

SITE Pierre-kleinhouse.com

BEHIND THE POSTERS: I absolutely love Tarantino's movies, and I feel that we share a common affection for mixing violence with fun. I wanted to create something bold, colorful, and dynamic that would really get attention and pop. Tarantino's movies have such a strong and well-known visual aspect to them, so I decided to create something different and free, representing his movies from my point of view.

INFLUENCES: So many influences, but Stanley Kubrick, Quentin Tarantino, and the Coen brothers are probably my favorite directors. As for art and illustration, I'm a big fan of Jeff Soto, The Weird Crew, Candy Killer, Brosmind, Steve Simpson, Herge, Mcbess, and anything connected to graffiti, street art, T-shirts, comics, manga, cartoons, and video games. Plus gig posters! I can look at gig posters for hours on end. A lot of my work is connected to music in one way or another. I always listen to music when I work, and I love creating music-related art and design.

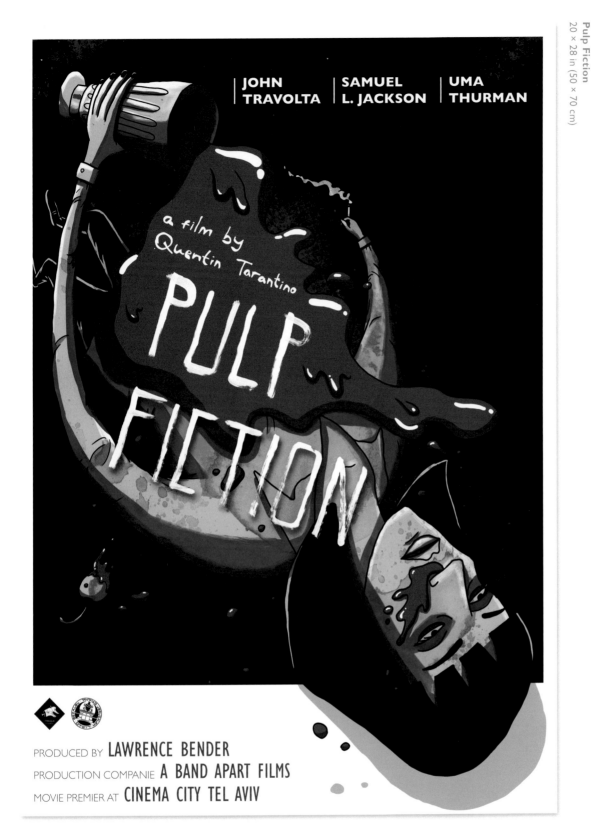

JOHN
TRAVOLTA | SAMUEL
L. JACKSON | UMA
THURMAN

a film by
Quentin Tarantino
PULP
FICTION

PRODUCED BY LAWRENCE BENDER
PRODUCTION COMPANIE A BAND APART FILMS
MOVIE PREMIER AT CINEMA CITY TEL AVIV

LOCATION Tel Aviv / Israel
SITE Pierre-kleinhouse.com

FAVORITE FILM / GENRE: No specific genre. Anything goes. My favorite films are *The Big Lebowski*, *The Matrix*, *Fight Club*, and of course *Reservoir Dogs*, *Pulp Fiction*, and *Inglourious Basterds*.

FIRST FILM: The *Teenage Mutant Ninja Turtles* '90s trilogy is the earliest that I can remember. My brother and I were obsessed with these kind of movies as kids. We used to watch superhero movies and cartoons like *Spider-Man* and *TMNT* for hours. As a teenager I discovered *Dragon Ball Z* and the world of anime and manga. It absolutely blew my mind. This was one of the reasons I initially became an illustrator. The fear of growing up is a powerful thing.

PREFERRED MEDIUM: I'm a big computer geek, so digital is usually how I roll. Sometimes it enables me to easily make short animations or gif animations, which is great. I always start with a fairly ugly pencil sketch, but most of the work is done on the computer. When creating posters I tend to work with a limited color palette so I can make silkscreen prints later.

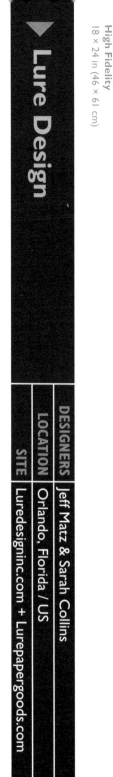

High Fidelity
18 × 24 in (46 × 61 cm)

DESIGNERS Jeff Matz & Sarah Collins

LOCATION Orlando, Florida / US

SITE Luredesigninc.com + Lurepapergoods.com

BEHIND THE POSTERS: Jeff: Enzian Theater is a client of ours. We handle the marketing materials for both the theater and the Florida Film Festival (which they produce). We've been making posters for their Cult Classics series with our pal, Billy Davis, for a few years now and these two films came up in the roster. I loved *High Fidelity* when I first saw it, so I was psyched for the poster. My first thought was to design a record label for "Top 5" records and incorporate the film title and show info. The second thought was to create the look of record spines that would fill the poster. I realized that something had to go on those spines and it struck me that it would fun to take the classic opening monologue, break it into pieces, and use that as the type on the spines. We're DIY printers, so I tried to build simple color breaks in four-color process that—for the most part—would look like solid colors.

Sarah: I've always loved the boundless imagination of *Labyrinth*, but I knew right away that I wanted to have a modern take here. The idea came quickly to build the title out of the labyrinth itself. The night of the film screening, *Labyrinth* fans quickly let us know that this interpretation was *not* what they were looking for! No punches were thrown, but awkward questions about the missing Bowie and Muppets followed.

RECENT PROJECTS: Jeff: The bulk of our work at Lure is corporate-related: identity, web design, advertising, and print collateral. We've been doing fun work for Shutterfly the last couple of years. We also have a line of screen printed note cards and journals that we create in-house under the name Lure Paper Goods.

Labyrinth
18 × 24 in (46 × 61 cm)

▼ Lure Design

DESIGNERS Jeff Matz & Sarah Collins
LOCATION Orlando, Florida / US
SITE Luredesigninc.com + Lurepapergoods.com

Sarah: We sometimes claim to be a "Jekyll and Hyde" studio, where on one side we handle advertising, books, brochures, identity, and interactive, and on our edgier side we create screen printed posters and paper goods. I love working for the Enzian Theater, and having full creative freedom on our cards and posters for Lure Paper Goods is pretty rad as well.

PINCH ME MOMENT: Jeff: It's always a thrill to get our posters published in design annuals or books. A few years back, Mary Stuart Masterson attended the Florida Film Festival and really liked our work. She asked us to design a poster for a movie she was directing. We also had a successful pop-up shop at a cool little gallery in Tampa called Workspace.

Sarah: Recently I was scrolling through my favorite design blog and my *Life Aquatic* poster came up. Those are the moments that make me smile. A fan also got a chest tattoo of one of my posters. That was a first.
IS THE FILM INDUSTRY COMING ALONG? Jeff: We're pretty disconnected from the film industry. We design posters more for fun than anything else. It's a creative outlet.

Sarah: As Jeff said, since we create film posters mostly for our local art house, we don't have much exposure to the industry. However, I have seen our design pals create posters for the industry and I hope this trend comes our way as well!
CLIENTS: Wilco, Treat, Old 97s, Shutterfly, Florida Film Festival.

LOCATION Pittsburgh, Pennsylvania / US

SITE jimrugg.com

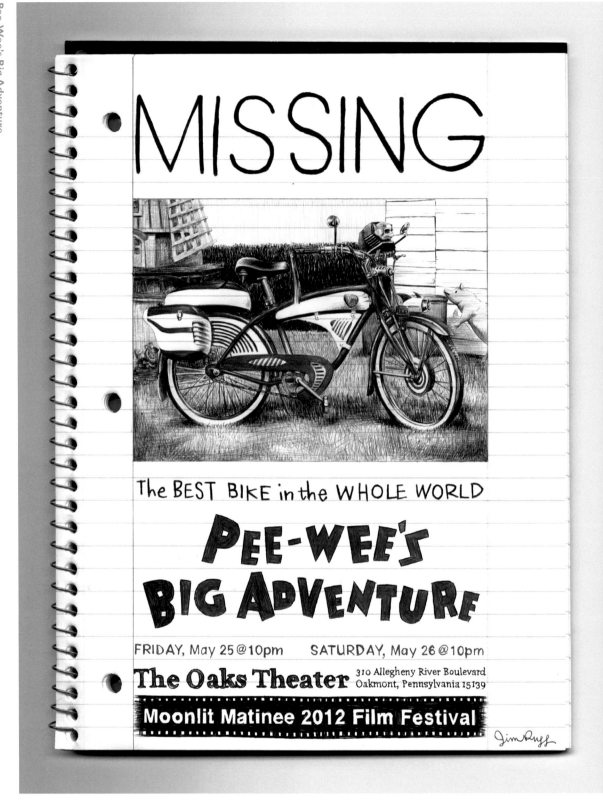

BEHIND THE POSTERS: *Pee-Wee's Big Adventure.* I made this poster for a local theater's "Midnight Matinee" series. The lost/missing flier concept immediately came to mind based on the movie plot. Once I made the prints, I stapled a few to telephone poles in the neighborhood around the theater.

Drive. I saw a print of this movie in a second-run theater and loved the way it looked, especially the color and lighting. The film is steeped in '80s style, which I associate with video game arcades I knew as a kid. In terms of color, era, and concept, the two seemed like a good match.

INFLUENCES: My influences are all over the place. I love movies, movie posters, and VHS box art. I make comics, so cartoonists like Dan Clowes, Chris Ware, Frank Miller, Jack Kirby, and Fort Thunder have been huge influences. I like a lot of filmmakers, too; Stanley Kubrick, Quentin Tarantino, Wes Anderson, Martin Scorsese, and the Coen brothers are some favorites.

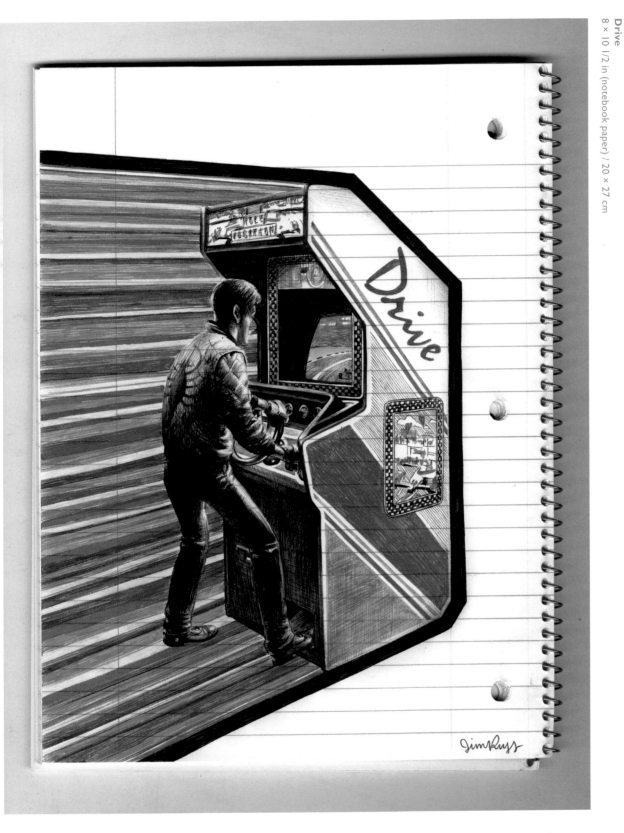

LOCATION Pittsburgh, Pennsylvania / US

SITE jimrugg.com

FAVORITE FILM / GENRE: I could never name just one. *Bottle Rocket* was a favorite for a while. I really like *A Serious Man*. Recent movies that I have enjoyed include *Under the Skin*, *Bones Brigade: An Autobiography*, and *Grand Budapest Hotel*. My favorite genre is comedy.

FIRST FILM: *King Kong* or *The Wizard of Oz*. I think *E.T.* was the first movie I saw in a theater.

PREFERRED MEDIUM: Pencil, ink, paper.

CLIENTS: ESPN, Harcourt, Disney, Marvel, DC Comics, Converse, Smirnoff, *New York* magazine, *LA Weekly*, iam8bit.

Day of the Dead
8 × 11 in (20 × 28 cm)

DESIGN FIRM	The Dude Designs
LOCATION	London / UK
SITE	Thedudedesigns.com

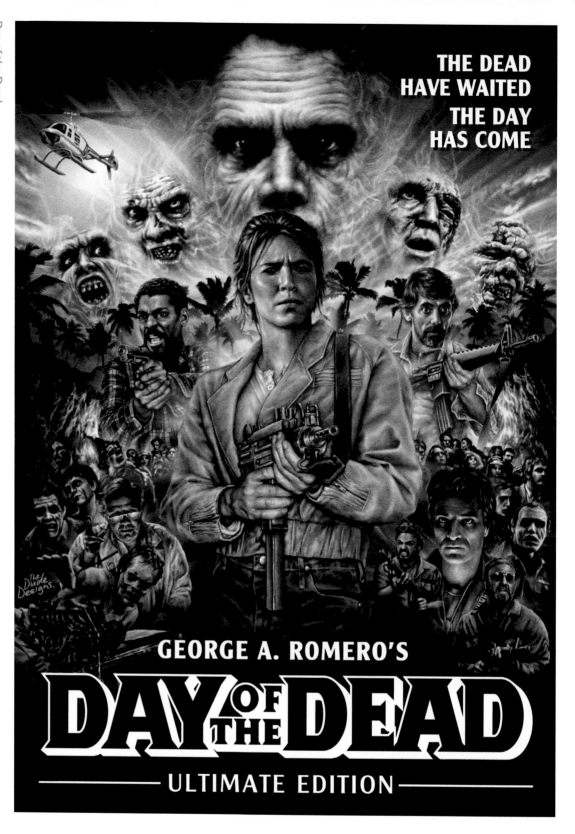

THE DEAD
HAVE WAITED
THE DAY
HAS COME

GEORGE A. ROMERO'S

DAY OF THE DEAD

— ULTIMATE EDITION —

BEHIND THE POSTERS: It was a treat to work on *Day of the Dead*, as I love the film. The characters and human nature in the film, as in all of Romero's zombie flicks, are really the central focus of the movie. The zombies, while a large part of the setting and plot, are represented as more of an outside attacking force. Romero's human characters, however, who are thrown into the zombie "pressure cooker," become the true horror of "The Dead" movies. With that in mind, I wanted to bring the central characters to the forefront of this piece. The main female protagonist, Sarah (Lori Cardille), is at the center of the action here. She is a brilliant, strong female character who I feel tends to get excluded from *Day of the Dead* artwork in favor of the zombies. She is a rare female horror lead who is not sexualized in the story, so I wanted to present her with a sense of dignity and steadfast quality. Sarah is backed up

by the brilliant characters of John and William, and these three individuals together represent the human heroes of *Day of the Dead*.

I gave *Savage Streets* a real '80s VHS cover vibe mixed with a classic action poster montage structure. There had only been six different designs created for past *Savage Streets* releases, so I wanted to inject a little something different with my version. Watching the film, there were one (or two) big things that jumped out at me. I had never seen such an indulgent use of breasts in a film since seeing an episode of *Benny Hill*. From Linda Blair bouncing down the street during the intro, to the gym class workout, to the shower fight scene . . . I could go on! So I wanted this piece to have an '80s action film meets tacky '80s sexploitation vibe. I reflected this in the color scheme, Linda's baby doll pout, and the big porn hair. I admit it might be heavy on the sex, but I felt this was a big part of the film, and it was an avenue for the design that hadn't been explored previously.

Savage Streets
8 × 11 in (20 × 28 cm)

Tom Hodge

DESIGN FIRM | The Dude Designs
LOCATION | London / UK
SITE | Thedudedesigns.com

What they did to her little sister was worse than a crime...

Now witness the ultimate execution

Savage Streets

Starring Linda Blair

INFLUENCES: I have largely been inspired by the '80s/'90s video cover artists who worked for Medusa, New Dimension, Guild, Entertainment in Video, Vestron Video, and New World Video, to name a few. The kings are Enzo Sciotti and Renato Casaro. Their work was just epic! Also, Claudio Casaro (Renato's son) was incredible, plus Laurent Melki and J.R. Gilkes. Sadly, it is difficult to track down video cover artists, since most VHS covers were nameless pieces.

FAVORITE FILM / GENRE: I burn through a lot of fun trash films. I'm a mad VHS addict and any obscure '80s horror, action, or sci-fi will catch my eye, such as *Neon Maniacs*, *Remote Control*, *Wild Thing*, *Rolling Vengeance*, and *Black Roses*. But my all-time favorites are *Alien*, *The Thing*, *Night of the Living Dead*, *The Shining*, *Phase IV*, *Death Wish 3*, and *Smokey and the Bandit* (or anything with Burt Reynolds in it). More recent favorites include *Session 9*, *Pontypool*, and *Insidious*.

CLIENTS: I mostly work on independent films, often to help them pick up distribution and for subsequent promotions. I have also worked with larger companies including 20th Century Fox, Magnet, Mondo, MPI Media, Oscilloscope, Dark Sky Pictures, Glass Eye Pix, Troma, Epic Pictures, Kino, Shout Factory, Koch Media, Arrow Video, CineCoup, Monster Pictures, Calibre Media, Polluted Pictures, 84 Entertainment, Big World Pictures, Death Waltz Records, and Arcade Pictures.

99

M. Fersner

Rock 'n' Roll High School
11 × 17 in (28 × 43 cm)

ALIAS HagCult

LOCATION Knoxville, Tennessee / US

SITE Hagcult.com

BEHIND THE POSTERS: The *Rock 'n' Roll High School* piece was for Hero Complex Gallery's "Kings of Cult: An Art Tribute to Roger Corman and Joe Dante." Being a huge fan of both directors and of the Ramones, I thought a tribute piece for *Rock 'n' Roll High School* would be incredibly fun. The Ramones were one of my first favorite bands. As a teen, I remember listening to them religiously every night before I passed out, and then waking up with my headphones still on. I tried to capture the energy and vibe of the music and film with this illustration. I think that being such a fan really shows in this piece. I created *The Rats in the Walls* piece for Bernie Wrightson and Steve Niles' "Something Spooky" show at Guzu Gallery. Being a fan of H. P. Lovecraft, I wanted to take one of his short stories and create my own imagery. [*The Rats in the Walls* was later the basis for the film *Necronomicon*.]

100

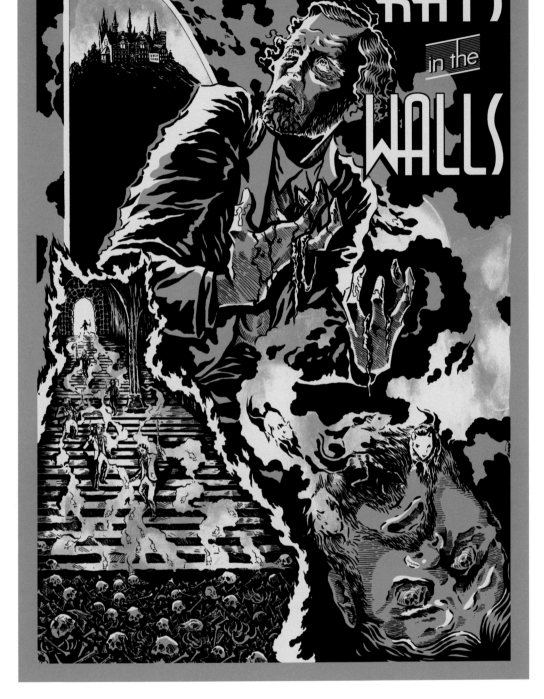

ALIAS	HagCult
LOCATION	Knoxville, Tennessee / US
SITE	Hagcult.com

INFLUENCES: My biggest influences are illustrators J. C. Leyendecker and Stephen Gammell. I grew up reading the *Scary Stories to Tell in the Dark* books and remember being horrified, yet in total awe of the illustrations. The terrifying and effective storytelling that Gammell demonstrated in his pieces is something I strive to achieve. As far as inspirational film directors go, I would choose Sergio Leone and Tod Browning. I have watched their movies endlessly and studied their use of lighting, settings, and atmospherics, trying to capture a similar effect in my illustrations.

FAVORITE FILM / GENRE: It would definitely be a split between classic horror and spaghetti westerns.
PREFERRED MEDIUM: Ink and acrylic.
CLIENTS: Hero Complex Gallery, Guzu Gallery, Gallery 1988.

Matt Ferguson

LOCATION	Sheffield / UK
SITE	Cakesandcomics.com

Guardians of the Galaxy
24 × 36 in (61 × 91 cm)

BEHIND THE POSTERS: In the *Guardians of the Galaxy* poster, the film looked to be Marvel's *Star Wars*, so it was obvious to do a poster directly inspired by the classic Jung one sheet. *Dawn of the Planet of the Apes* was a reaction to the trailer for that particular film. I thought it looked amazing and loved that the film was showing apes as a new society (supplanting humans), so I tried to convey this concept in my poster.

INFLUENCES: Ridley Scott, Steven Spielberg, and Stanley Kubrick have all had a huge influence. John Carpenter is particularly responsible for how I go about creating posters. I love the economy and no-nonsense of his films. However, I am influenced by so many pop culture artists that it is not fair to list just a few.

FAVORITE FILM / GENRE: Science fiction.
FIRST FILM: *Flash Gordon* (I was actually born to that film!)
PREFERRED MEDIUM: Digital.

CLIENTS: Marvel, Disney, 20th Century Fox, Paramount, Universal, Bottleneck Gallery, Gallery 1988, Hero Complex Gallery.

Blood Bath
8 × 12 in (21 × 30 cm)

William Dalebout

DESIGN FIRM Pushbutton Studio
LOCATION Shanghai / China
SITE Behance.net/pushbuttonstudio.com

THE SHRIEKING OF MUTILATED VICTIMS CAGED IN A BLACK PIT OF HORROR!

BLOOD BATH

WILLIAM CAMPBELL   MARISSA MATHES   LINDA SAUNDERS

BEHIND THE POSTERS: *Blood Bath* started out as just an illustration of a girl in a tub, which I later converted into a movie poster. I still haven't seen *Blood Bath*, but it looks awful. I chose *Bride of the Monster* after watching the film. It's so bizarre and obscure and bad that I thought it needed a poster.

INFLUENCES: Tara McPherson, Steve Simpson, Marcos Chin, Brandon Johnson, and Catherine Dedova.
FAVORITE FILM / GENRE: I prefer older movies. The '70s and '80s were the pinnacle of American filmmaking, and CGI effects don't interest me at all (. . . blech).

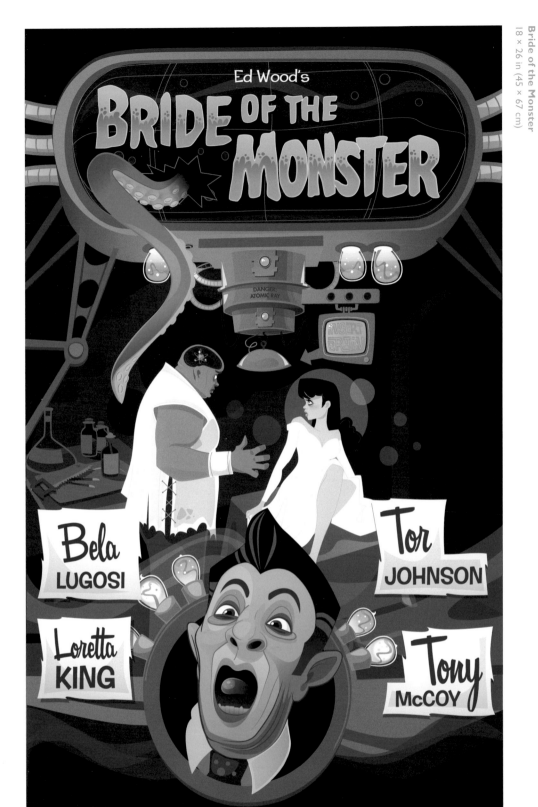

Bride of the Monster
18 × 26 in (45 × 67 cm)

William Dalebout

DESIGN FIRM	Pushbutton Studio
LOCATION	Shanghai / China
SITE	Behance.net/pushbuttonstudio.com

FIRST FILM: *Star Trek: The Motion Picture*. Still the only decent *Star Trek* film.
PREFERRED MEDIUM: I work almost exclusively in vector. It's an interesting medium with unique abilities and limitations.

CLIENTS: Blue Cross, Disney, Coca Cola, Pipilu (Beijing), Bobbi Brown, App Annie.

Mathias Valdez

Rosemary's Baby
24 × 36 in (61 × 91 cm)
A Blunt Graffix release

DESIGN FIRM	LastLeaf Printing & Design
LOCATION	Pueblo, Colorado / US
SITE	Lastleafprinting.com

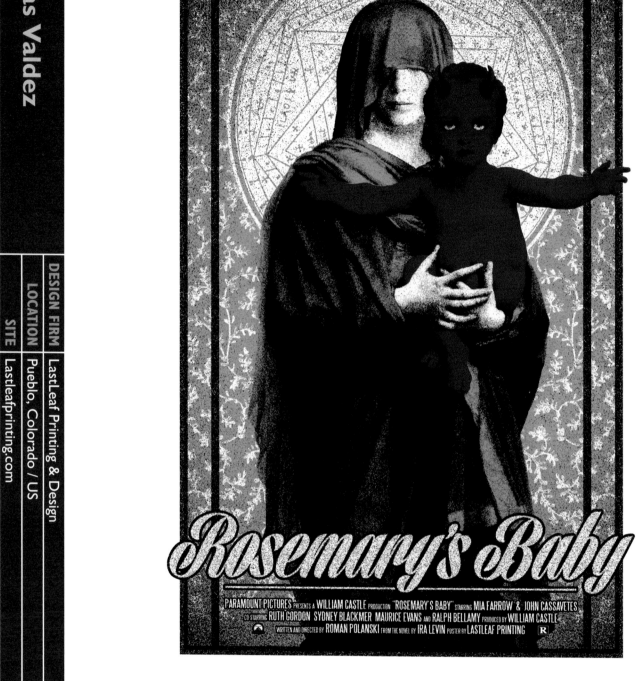

BEHIND THE POSTERS: My friend Matt from Blunt Graffix asked me to do both of these pieces (and a few more) for screenings at the Bijou Metro Theater in Eugene, Oregon. The theater joins up with the Eugene Film Society to host screenings of classic and cult films outside their normal new release schedule. Very cool place.

INFLUENCES: I draw from lots of different folks. Print Mafia, Rob Jones, and Art Chantry, to name a few. Some of the greats, in my opinion. **FAVORITE FILM / GENRE:** Horror, all the way.

Dazed and Confused
24 × 36 in (61 × 91 cm)
A Blunt Graffix release

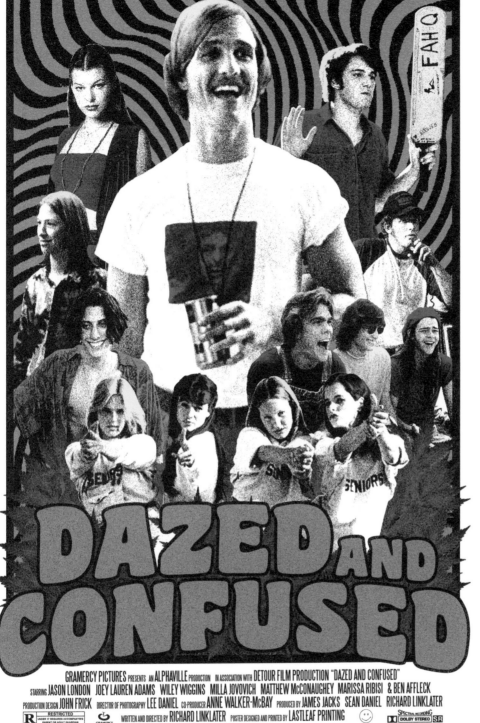

GRAMERCY PICTURES PRESENTS AN ALPHAVILLE PRODUCTION IN ASSOCIATION WITH DETOUR FILM PRODUCTION "DAZED AND CONFUSED"
STARRING JASON LONDON   JOEY LAUREN ADAMS   WILEY WIGGINS   MILLA JOVOVICH   MATTHEW McCONAUGHEY   MARISSA RIBISI   & BEN AFFLECK
PRODUCTION DESIGN JOHN FRICK   DIRECTOR OF PHOTOGRAPHY LEE DANIEL   CO-PRODUCER ANNE WALKER-McBAY   PRODUCED BY JAMES JACKS   SEAN DANIEL   RICHARD LINKLATER
WRITTEN AND DIRECTED BY RICHARD LINKLATER   POSTER DESIGNED AND PRINTED BY LASTLEAF PRINTING

FIRST FILM: That's a hard one to answer. It's like asking if I remember the first song I ever heard. I have been immersed in film, music, and art for as long as I can remember.
PREFERRED MEDIUM: Screen printing.

CLIENTS: I have spent most of my career doing gig posters for bands like the Avett Brothers, Alabama Shakes, Mudhoney, and many more. In the last year I have slowly moved toward creating more film posters, which is awesome because I am a huge cinephile.

SELF-IMPROVEMENT *masturbation*
SELF-DESTRUCTION IS THE *answer*

BEHIND THE POSTERS: In 2010 I started an illustration series titled "52 Bad Dudes," where every Friday I would post up a new illustration of a "bad dude" that was submitted to me. Tyler was week #30 and Edward was week #31.

INFLUENCES: Any of the artists featured at Mondo. There are many more that I briefly looked at during Art History 101.

FAVORITE FILM / GENRE: If I am answering this purely from a non-statistical sort of way, I'm going to go with *Life of Pi*. If it's considered by number of plays, it's likely going to be *Kung Pow: Enter the Fist*.

Adam Sidwell

LOCATION Seattle, Washington / US
SITE Adamsidwell.com

Fight Club
18 × 24 in (46 × 61 cm)

This is your life
Ending one minute at a time

FIRST FILM: The first and only film to remember, *The Transformers: The Movie* (that is actually the name). The one where Optimus Prime rips out his heart and gives it to that immature teenage Hot Rod dick.
PREFERRED MEDIUM: I usually work with pencils and/or India ink and then tighten it up in Photoshop.

ADDITIONAL REMARKS: His name is Robert Paulson.

Cannibal Holocaust
24 × 36 in (61 × 91 cm)
A Grey Matter Art release

BEHIND THE POSTERS: For *Only God Forgives* [right], AllCity Media wanted to team up to create a poster. Everyone was happy with the results, including director Nicolas Winding Refn. For *Cannibal Holocaust*, Grey Matter Art asked me to be the very first artist for their print releases, and in a ballsy move decided to come right out of the gate with one of the most notoriously controversial films ever made. Kudos to them for taking the chance!

INFLUENCES: I am heavily influenced by coffee and coffee alone.
FAVORITE FILM / GENRE: *Breakin' with the Mighty Poppalots.*

Only God Forgives
24 × 36 in (61 × 91 cm)
An AllCity release

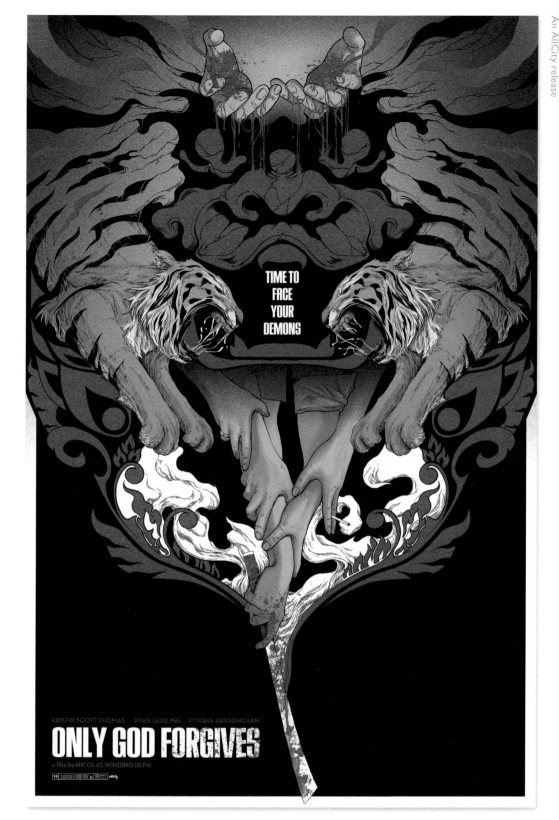

FIRST FILM: *Twincest Vol. 26.*
PREFERRED MEDIUM: Scraped tartar buildup diluted in my tears.

CLIENTS: Randy Savage, Elmer's Glue, Drake's left eyebrow.
ADDITIONAL REMARKS: Cats rule everything around me.

Mad Max 2
36 × 24 in (91 × 61 cm)

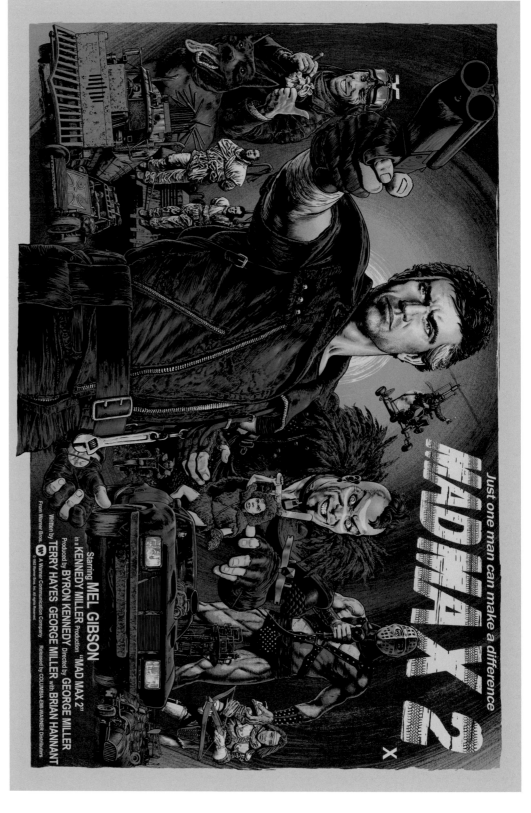

LOCATION Eastbourne, England / UK

SITE Chrisweston.com

BEHIND THE POSTERS: Both posters were chosen from a list of suggestions presented by a silkscreen print commissioning group. *The Good, the Bad, and the Ugly* has always been one of my favorite films. I also wasn't impressed with the original film poster and felt there was an opportunity to provide a decent alternative.

INFLUENCES: Moebius, Drew Struzan, Brian Bysouth, Francois Schuiten, Brian Bolland, Frank Hampson, Sergio Toppi, and Robert McGinnis.
FAVORITE FILM / GENRE: *The Sound of Music.*
FIRST FILM: *Lost Horizon* (1973).

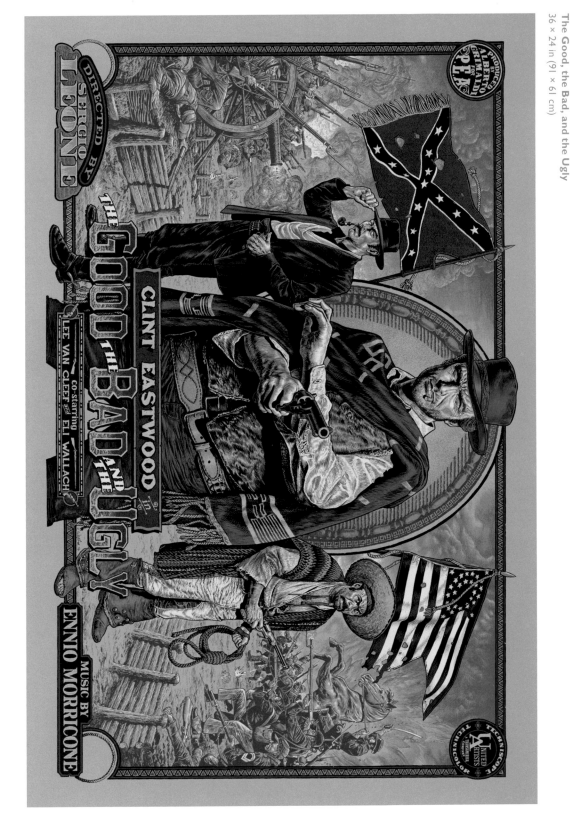

▼ **Chris Weston**

| LOCATION | Eastbourne, England / UK |
| SITE | Chrisweston.com |

ADDITIONAL REMARKS: I am grateful for the opportunity to create alternative film posters. Like most people, I am sick to death of the prevailing trend for anodyne, Photoshopped film posters, so it's pleasing to see an underground poster scene provide a thriving and exciting alternative. I am a huge fan of 1970s hand-painted film posters and am slowly amassing a collection of classics. I am particularly partial to the Roger Moore-era *James Bond* posters, and my aim is to create art that gives me the same thrill that I used to receive when I gazed at the McGinnis-painted quads outside of my local flea pit of a cinema.

Tinker Tailor Soldier Spy
24 × 36 in (61 × 91 cm)

DESIGN FIRM helloMuller
LOCATION London / UK
SITE Hellomuller.com

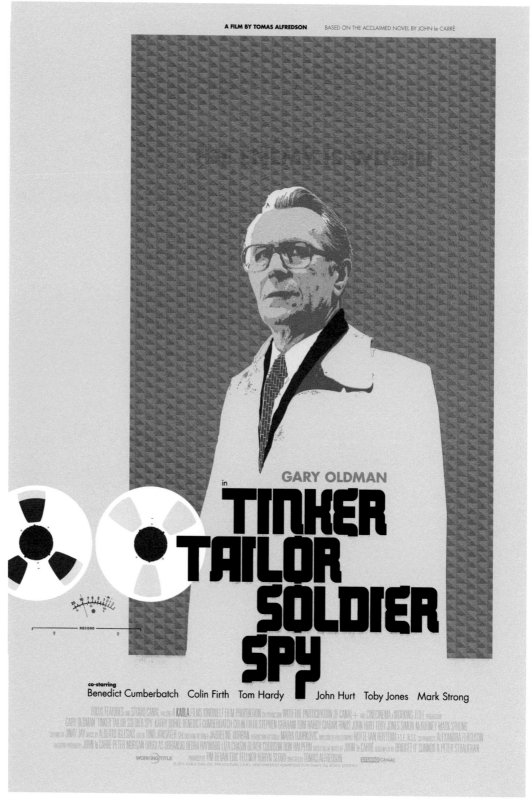

BEHIND THE POSTERS: *Tinker Tailor Soldier Spy* was a self-initiated, unpublished project. I was inspired by how perfectly the film captures '70s interior design and wanted to highlight the orange meeting pod in the poster. I also wanted to revive the typography of the novel's first printing —and celebrate iconic poster designs from that era, especially *The Conversation*, while adding subtle layers in the design to illustrate the narrative of the film [see the hidden text in the background]. *ShortList* magazine commissioned the *Gravity* poster. I wanted to step away from focusing on Sandra Bullock's character, and rather use the canvas of the poster to emphasize the emptiness of space (framing the core idea of the film).

INFLUENCES: Stanley Kubrick, Katsuhiro Otomo, Massimo Vignelli, Christopher Nolan, George Lucas, Total Design, Syd Mead, Bob Peak, John Alvin, Lou Dorfsmann.
FAVORITE FILM / GENRE: I am a massive sci-fi fan. I can watch *2001: A Space Odyssey* time and again. But I also have a soft spot for *Close Encounters of the Third Kind*, *Logan's Run*, *Brainstorm*, *The Black Hole*, and *Blade Runner*.

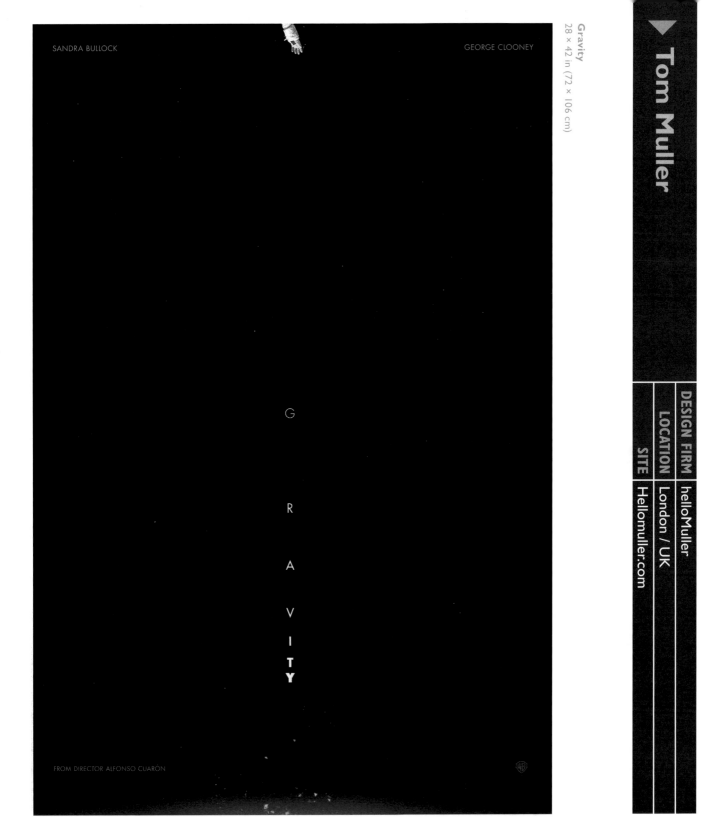

SANDRA BULLOCK

GEORGE CLOONEY

G

R

A

V

I

T

Y

FROM DIRECTOR ALFONSO CUARÓN

Gravity
28 × 42 in (72 × 106 cm)

▼ Tom Muller

DESIGN FIRM	helloMuller
LOCATION	London / UK
SITE	Hellomuller.com

FIRST FILM: It is probably a coin toss between *Close Encounters* and *Superman: The Movie*.
PREFERRED MEDIUM: I work primarily across print and digital, interchangeably, but lately I've been doing more print design.

CLIENTS: Image Comics, DC Entertainment, Valiant Entertainment, *Wired*, Samsung, StudioCanal, Glass Eye, Protozoa Pictures, WGSN, Sony Electronics, Flipboard, *TV Guide*.

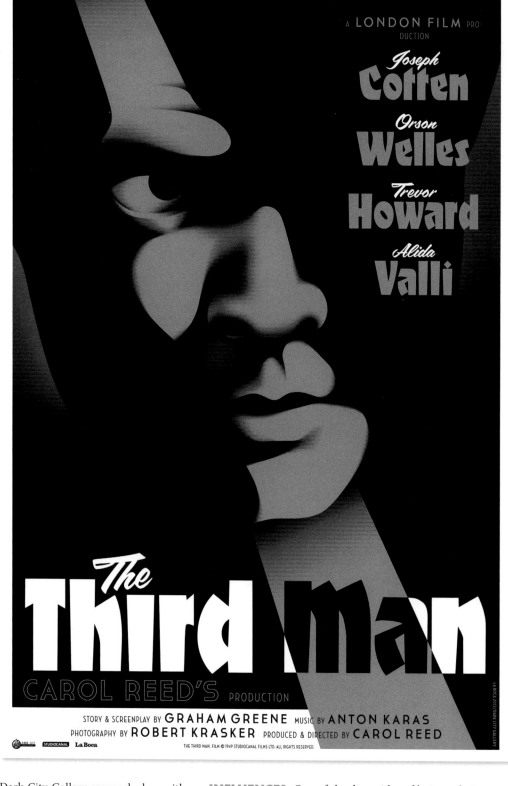

Scot Bendall

The Third Man
24 × 36 in (61 × 91 cm)
A Dark City Gallery release

DESIGN FIRM La Boca

LOCATION London /UK & Amsterdam / The Netherlands

SITE Laboca.co.uk

BEHIND THE POSTERS: Dark City Gallery approached us with the idea of creating a poster for *The Third Man* as part of their "British Cinema" collection. We have a great affection for all things art deco at the studio, so we jumped at the chance to create artwork for such an iconic film. It was actually the first screen printed film poster we produced and were grateful that Dark City gave us the opportunity.
For *King Kong* it was the opposite situation. We had an idea that we'd like to celebrate *King Kong*'s eightieth anniversary, so we approached Dark City with the idea. They were keen to produce the poster with us.

INFLUENCES: One of the downsides of being a designer is that it's often difficult to switch off and stop looking for inspiration. Therefore we find that our influences often derive from the most unlikeliest of sources. It may sound obvious, but I think it's vital to remain inspired by a very broad experience and it's something that I try to embrace. If I attempted to write a list of influences it would almost be never-ending, as there is so much to celebrate.

116

King Kong
24 × 36 in (61 × 91 cm)
A Dark City Gallery release

DESIGN FIRM La Boca
LOCATION London /UK & Amsterdam / The Netherlands
SITE Laboca.co.uk

KING KONG

La Boca

THE BEAST LOOKED UPON THE FACE OF BEAUTY AND IT STAYED ITS HAND FROM KILLING

LA BOCA 2013/DARK CITY GALLERY

FAVORITE FILM / GENRE: I have a preference for sci-fi and anything on the stranger side of normal. I also have an unhealthy fascination with post-apocalyptic movies. I can't explain why. Wishful thinking, perhaps. A film that I seem to refer to often is *The Holy Mountain* by Alejandro Jodorowsky. That's probably my next dream poster project if someone offers us the chance.

FIRST FILM: As a child of the '80s, my earliest memories of film most certainly evolve around Disney. Back then every Disney release was a big deal to a kid! I still have quite a few of the picture disc sound tracks that you could buy at the theater. However, *E.T.* was the first film release that I remember getting totally hyped about.

PREFERRED MEDIUM: Almost everything that we produce is digital. We sketch ideas in the initial stages but ultimately transfer them to a Mac. We then use Wacom tablets and a combination of Adobe Illustrator and Photoshop to create the final artwork.

CLIENTS: We're fortunate to have the opportunity to work on a variety of different projects and for a wide range of clients, from small independents to huge multinationals. In addition to film posters, we design record covers, books, advertising campaigns, and any other fun stuff that comes our way. In the past we've worked with 20th Century Fox, Warner Bros., Universal, Sony, Adidas, Nike, Google, Ray Ban, Volkswagen, and many more.

ADDITIONAL REMARKS: Don't believe the hype.

Jayson Weidel

Fantastic Mr. Fox
(actual title = *Mr. Cussin' Fox*)
18 × 24 in (41 × 61 cm)

DESIGN FIRM	Oo-De-Lally
LOCATION	Dayton, Ohio / US
SITE	Oo-De-Lally.com

BEHIND THE POSTERS: I created *Mr. Cussin' Fox* for a Wes Anderson-themed show, choosing to base it on *The Fantastic Mr. Fox* because it was the only Wes Anderson film that I was a fan of. More specifically, I was a fan of the book first and the movie second. *Mars Attacks* was made for a gallery show with the theme "Retro Sci-Fi Laser Guns and Weapons." I wasn't around when the Topps *Mars Attacks* cards came out in the '60s, so my connection with the property was purely Tim Burton's film. No guns are featured here, but as everyone knows, lasers are abundant in the *Mars Attacks* world.

INFLUENCES: My influences are all over the place. Alex Ross is a big one, plus Drew Struzan, Adam Hughes, Tim Burton, and Walt Disney. I am always striving to improve my technique, and when I see their work it just fuels me.

DESIGN FIRM Oo-De-Lally
LOCATION Dayton, Ohio / US
SITE Oo-De-Lally.com

FAVORITE FILM / GENRE: My favorite genre is comic book films. Marvel has done a great job translating their characters to the big screen. I cannot wait to see how DC handles the *Justice League* and all of their individual films. Outside of this, the modern classics of course, such as the *Star Wars* and *Indiana Jones* films. Basically if Drew Struzan painted the related one sheet it's on my list. *Pee-Wee's Big Adventure* is a guilty pleasure and is by far my favorite film of all time. I've seen it a thousand times.

FIRST FILM: The first film that I ever saw in the theater was *E.T.* After that I think it was *The Empire Strikes Back*.
PREFERRED MEDIUM: Gouache paints for my traditional side, and when I am on the computer I prefer to use Adobe Illustrator.
CLIENTS: My day job is in advertising and I work with Dark Hall Mansion here and there. I also take on quite a few commissions.

Carrie
16 × 24 in (41 × 61 cm)
An Odd City Entertainment release

DESIGN FIRM | Jessica Deahl Illustration
LOCATION | Austin, Texas / US
SITE | Jessicadeahl.com

BEHIND THE POSTERS: I created the *Carrie* poster as a commission for Odd City Entertainment out of Austin. Odd City saw my work in a few pop art shows and had the license for the original 1976 film. I was immediately on board. The film was one of the first horror movies that I remember seeing as a child, and I have always been a sucker for Stephen King books and film adaptations. I also loved the idea of taking on a film with a strong female lead.

Many other *Carrie* film posters have focused on the iconic prom scene. However, for me the real heart of the film stems from Carrie's life at home and her interactions with her oppressive mother. It feels like a

triumph when she finally takes control of her destiny and breaks free from the abuse. In my piece, blood drips from her hands down to her home, alluding to a puppet master/puppet relationship. Carrie is often seen as a horrifying figure, but I find her heroic.

My *Coming to America* print was created for a Gallery 1988 "Product Placement" show. Screen print artists were tasked with creating pieces inspired by products from our favorite movies. My mind went right to "Soul Glo." I have a real affinity for 1980s Eddie Murphy films. They are equal parts smart and silly, and oh-so-quotable. The "Soul Glo" product almost plays its own role in *Coming to America*, from that amazingly

Coming to America
18 × 24 in (46 × 61 cm)

Jessica Deahl

DESIGN FIRM	Jessica Deahl Illustration
LOCATION	Austin, Texas / US
SITE	Jessicadeahl.com

soulful jheri curl commercial to advertisements behind the actors in the barbershop. It was a lot of fun to revisit that film and create what I would imagine as the real "Soul Glo" advertisement pasted on the streets of Queens. All of the swirly hair was fun to draw and ink, and I added some distress and intentional misregistration to make it feel a little rough around the edges.

INFLUENCES: Wes Anderson, Stanley Kubrick, Sylvain Chomet, Charley Harper, Charles and Ray Eames, Egon Schiele.

FAVORITE FILM / GENRE: Independent, drama/comedy.

FIRST FILM: *The Last Unicorn.*

PREFERRED MEDIUM: Screen print, pen, and ink.

CLIENTS: NBC (*Saturday Night Live*), AMC (*Breaking Bad*), Gallery 1988, Odd City Entertainment, *MovieMaker* magazine, *The Austin Chronicle*, and The Fillmore (San Francisco).

ADDITIONAL REMARKS: The world of licensed and inspired poster art is incredible and ever-evolving. Creating poster art has provided a way for us as fans to pay homage and give new life to some of our favorite film and television franchises. In turn, we get to share that love with art collectors and purveyors of the scene.

Hannibal
18 × 24 in (46 × 61 cm)

LOCATION Sunland, California / US

SITE Hanzelharo.tumblr.com

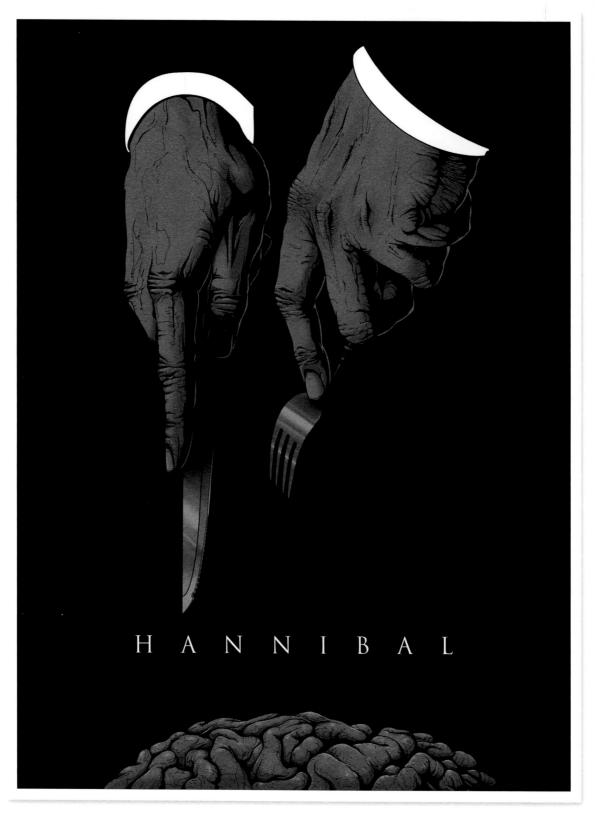

HANNIBAL

BEHIND THE POSTERS: *Hannibal* was my first solo design work on a larger scale [the artwork was used for the special edition DVD], so in that regard it's significant for me. One aspect of *Hannibal* that I love is the juxtaposition of horror and sophistication. Also, I had originally sketched the print to include Ray's head, but decided to keep the focus on "the act" itself.

Regarding *Pet Sematary*, a few years ago I tried to befriend a stray cat that was roaming my apartment building. Every day I would leave a bit of food in a bowl, moving it closer to my door. Over a few weeks the bowl made its way from the garage, to the stairs, to the first floor, and then to my front door. I finally moved the bowl just inside my apartment, but that's where my success ended. Even though I stayed at a safe distance, the cat refused to take that final step. Eventually I gave up, picked up the bowl, shut the door, turned down the lights, and sat down to watch a movie. After a couple of minutes, I heard a strange noise from beneath the entertainment center. I turned on the lamp, looked down, and there were a pair of glowing eyes looking back at me. Both the cat and I freaked out. The movie I was trying to watch was *Pet Sematary*. I didn't finish it then and haven't tried to watch it since.

INFLUENCES: My influences, on a conscious level, come mostly from other artists. Dave McKean, Eric Fortune, Kent Williams, Ian Francis, Wayshak, Horkey, and Laurent Durieux, to name a few, keep me going.

FAVORITE FILM / GENRE: I'm all about the sci-fi these days.

FIRST FILM: Growing up in Cuba, there weren't a lot of film options. Outings to the theater were few and far between. Most of the movies were either Russian stop-motion (masterpieces I'm sure, but for a kid, so boring) and the occasional cartoon of Cuba's iconic campesino El Pidio Valdez. Even though El Pidio was a propaganda cartoon about the Cuban independence war, at that age I found rifles, cannons, and machete warfare incredibly amusing. It still holds up to this day. Next to refugiados (guava and cheese pastry) it's the best thing to come out of Cuba. Then I saw anime on the big screen (the movie was *Space Firebird*). It was the first time that I walked out of a theater wanting to immediately return. I had no idea what the plot of *Space Firebird* was, but the animation blew my mind. At that moment I stopped my steady routine of drawing of tanks and started on the sci-fi path—a shame, really, because I had those tanks down tight.

PREFERRED MEDIUM: My weapons of choice are oils, but I try to diversify as often as possible. I've been working more these days with inks and digital.

123

The Terminator
18 × 24 in (46 × 61 cm)

ALIAS Electric Zombie

LOCATION Tampa, Florida / US

SITE Theelectriczombie.com + Get86d.com

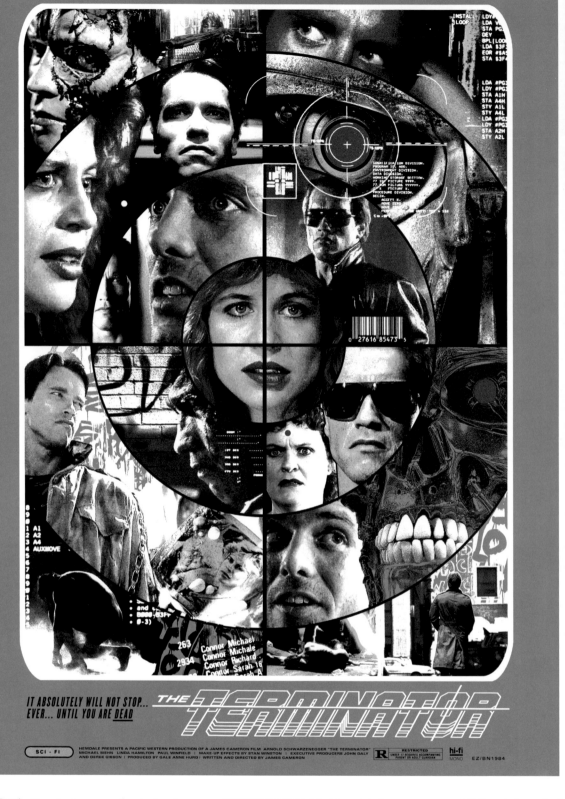

IT ABSOLUTELY WILL NOT STOP...
EVER... UNTIL YOU ARE **DEAD**

SCI·FI   HEMDALE PRESENTS A PACIFIC WESTERN PRODUCTION OF A JAMES CAMERON FILM ARNOLD SCHWARZENEGGER "THE TERMINATOR" MICHAEL BIEHN   LINDA HAMILTON   PAUL WINFIELD | MAKE-UP EFFECTS BY STAN WINSTON | EXECUTIVE PRODUCERS JOHN DALY AND DEREK GIBSON | PRODUCED BY GALE ANNE HURD | WRITTEN AND DIRECTED BY JAMES CAMERON   R RESTRICTED   hi-fi MONO   EZ/BN1984

BEHIND THE POSTERS: *The Terminator* came about when I was asked to be part of a Bottleneck Gallery's "It Came from 1984" show. This was a *huge* year for films. I am primarily known for horror, so I wanted to do something a bit different and went with *Terminator*. I colored the poster with color schemes from the shirt that Arnold took from the "street punk thug" in the film, and built the print around the idea of a target. The finished piece was printed on brushed metal card stock.

Teenage Mutant Ninja Turtles II was created for my clothing company, Electric Zombie. I released T-shirts, plus this print. Artists typically focus on the first *Turtles* film, but #2 was always my favorite. It was the most consumer-oriented, blatantly poppy, and easily the most fun of the franchise, so I made sure that the print conveyed this.

INFLUENCES: My biggest influence was my childhood. I watched wrestling every week, was into comic books and skateboarding, watched cartoons on Saturday (with a big bowl of Kix), and loved music. Being a kid was awesome.

My dad was also a big inspiration. If he hadn't bought me so many toys and "made" me watch scary movies with him, I probably wouldn't be where I am.

My artistic inspirations include Jason Edmiston, Tyler Stout, Clark Orr, Matthew Skiff, Shepard Fairey, Jack Kirby, and of course Jim Phillips. Director Robert Rodriguez is also high on my list. Rodriguez is so diverse. He can do kids, horror, and action movies, plus he edits, writes, directs, scores, and creates special effects.

Teenage Mutant Ninja Turtles II: The Secret of the Ooze
18 × 24 in (46 × 61 cm)

ALIAS	Electric Zombie
LOCATION	Tampa, Florida / US
SITE	Theelectriczombie.com + Get86d.com

FAVORITE FILM / GENRE: I love comic book movies. Horror used to be my favorite, but that genre has taken a downward plunge since the *Saw* franchise ended. The best horror movies that I've seen the past few years have included *The Collector*, *Mother's Day*, and *The Loved Ones*. However, these days horror movies are all about ghosts and being possessed, which doesn't do much for me.

FIRST FILM: I remember being taken to the movie theater to see *The Care Bears Movie*. I don't remember much of the movie, but recall leaving the theater and crying my eyes out because Dark Heart scared the shit out of me. However, the first movies I remember watching from beginning to end were *Teen Wolf* and *A Nightmare on Elm Street 3: Dream Warriors*. I actually lived on Elm Street back then, so the *Elm Street* films were a staple at my house. I also vividly remember watching *The Evil Dead* and *Monster Squad*. Let's just say that I had a cool dad.

CLIENTS: I primarily work in the music industry designing apparel, logos, and album artwork. My biggest clients have included Nirvana, Metallica, Billy Joel, Eminem, Blink-182, Avenged Sevenfold, Deftones, AC/DC, and Kiss.

Ridge Rooms

A Christmas Story
(actual title = *Only I Didn't Say "Fudge" …*)
18 × 24 in (46 × 61 cm)

LOCATION Millersburg, Ohio / US

SITE Ridgerooms.com

BEHIND THE POSTERS: When I received the list of films that we could choose from for Gallery 1988s "Crazy 4 Cult" show in 2013, *A Christmas Story* was right on top. I didn't go farther down the list before emailing back my choice. It's been one of my favorite films since I was a kid and I used to live in the neighborhood where the real house stands.

Scooby-Doo was for a gallery show called "Righteous Rides," and I mulled over quite a few iconic vehicles before landing on the Mystery Machine. I have a screen print series called "Spoilers," which uses glow-in-the-dark ink to show a hidden layer of art and plot twists in the piece. Scooby and the gang just seemed like a great fit, since the hidden layer

could reveal the people inside the costumes. [Author's note: since Scooby-Doo was eventually made into a feature film, we bent the rules here a bit. It's such a great piece that it deserved exposure.]

INFLUENCES: Charles Schulz, *The Far Side*, Alfred Hitchcock, mid-century advertising, *The Twilight Zone*, Chuck Jones, Radiohead, Hanna-Barbera, Roger Corman, classic television, and Ray Bradbury.

FAVORITE FILM / GENRE: My interests are all over the place, but I guess my desert island-style pick is what I call "caper cinema"—anything with a heist, a prison break, or both. *The Sting*, the original *The Italian Job*, anything Steve McQueen. I also love early slapstick comedies and film noir.

Ridge Rooms

LOCATION	Millersburg, Ohio / US
SITE	Ridgerooms.com

Scooby-Doo
(actual title = *Those Meddling Kids* / contains glow-in-the-dark ink)
16 × 12 in (41 × 30 cm)

FIRST FILM: I can't remember the first film that I went to (although I have a vivid memory of sobbing the whole way home from *E.T.*). I didn't get to see many films at the theater as a kid, so my "firsts" were all things broadcast on Sunday afternoons or late-night television: a lot of James Bond films, live-action Disney flicks from the '60s, and lots of '50s B-movies. *The Ghost and Mr. Chicken* was probably my first favorite film, along with anything with Gene Kelly in it. I was oddly obsessed with him in grade school.

PREFERRED MEDIUM: Adobe Illustrator for prints and colored pencil/colored paper for original drawings.

CLIENTS: Previously in-house at *Peanuts*, Barnes & Noble, and Pepsi. Fantasy clients: Turner Classic Movies, the *James Bond* franchise, Tom Hanks, and *The Simpsons*. I'd also like to get into creating some quirky gig posters.

ADDITIONAL REMARKS: I'm excited to move into a new pop art studio/showroom space. It's in a cute little Victorian tourist town in the Midwest. It's been quite a culture shock from living in huge cities the last two decades, but I never could have afforded to take this plunge somewhere like Brooklyn or Austin.

127

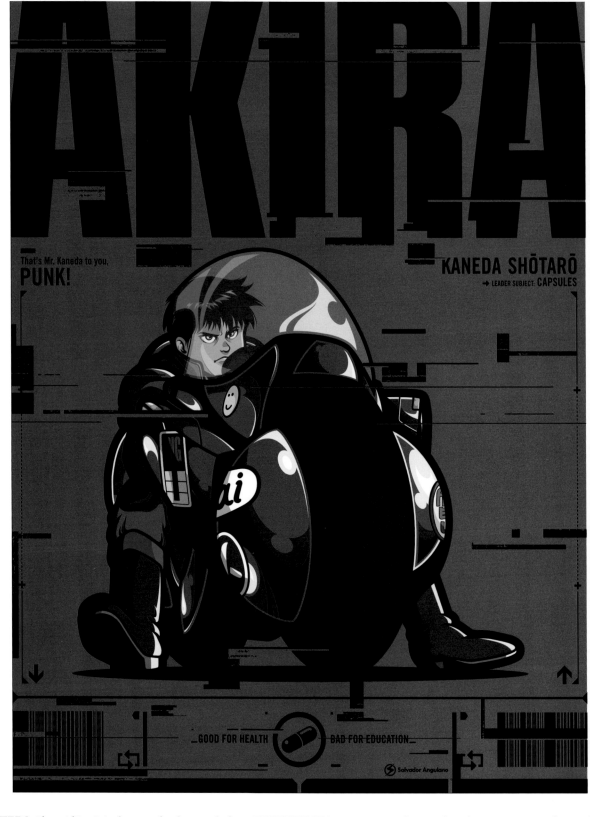

Salvador Anguiano

Akira
18 × 24 in (46 × 61 cm)

LOCATION León, GTO / Mexico

SITE Be.net/salvador

BEHIND THE POSTERS: I love *Akira*. It is almost as fundamental of an experience as *Star Wars*. The initial sequence always blows my mind; it's so violent, yet so beautifully crafted. I wanted to capture the cyberpunk feel of the movie in my print (i.e., some of the irreverence, plus the sheer coolness of Shotaro Kaneda).

Big Hero 6 was part of a Poster Posse project, and here I wanted to pay tribute to the Japanese side of the film (not to mention legendary studio Furi Furi) by using clean, crisp lines. I also injected some childish energy into Baymax.

INFLUENCES: I grew up watching *Robotech*, *Mazinger*, *Astroboy*, and *Gundam* (which I think shows in my work), and later a healthy dose of '80s action/adventure movies. As for artists, there's Paul Ainsworth, Robert Bruno, Doaly, Florey, Patrick Connan, Laurie Greasley and all of the Poster Posse guys—Matt Taylor, DKNG, James White (huge influence all around), Kendrick Kidd, Clark Orr, Christopher DeLorenzo . . . too many to mention.

Big Hero 6
18 × 24 in (46 × 61 cm)

LOCATION	León, GTO / Mexico
SITE	Be.net/salvador

FAVORITE FILM / GENRE: My favorite film changes depending on my mood. I have a few that I can watch over and over, including *Lost In Translation*, *High Fidelity*, *Hot Rod*, *Dazed and Confused*, and *Adventureland*. The '80s classics as well. My kid and I particularly love *Hot Rod*. It just never gets old for us.

FIRST FILM: *Star Wars*.

PREFERRED MEDIUM: Vector.

CLIENTS: I have a variety of clients, from small local brands (which I love to work with) to larger clients like Marvel, WWE, and Fox.

ADDITIONAL REMARKS: If you love creating art, keep at it. Keep working hard and don't be a d*ck. Thanks for the opportunity, and thanks to my lovely wife, who is everything to me.

Trafic
23 × 33 in (59 × 84 cm)

TRAFIC

UN FILM DE
JACQUES
TATI

EN COULEURES

BEHIND THE POSTERS: I saw both *Trafic* and *The 400 Blows* as a kid. Movies were always watched and then discussed with my family. Growing up in the '80s and due to VHS, I was exposed to a great variety of films at an early age. I watched *Trafic* with my father as part of a series of Jacques Tati films that was on television. Tati was a magical figure for me and I always viewed him as my uncle. He was from my grandfather's generation and I viewed his films as their "home movies," full of information about their earlier lives that I could only imagine from

photographs. Along with the obvious joy the films gave me, they instilled a sense of nostalgia, an appreciation for the things that came before and a longing to preserve them.

The 400 Blows remains one of my favorite movies of all time. I watched it by myself and I remember being proud for having tackled the film, instead of watching *Star Wars* or *Drunken Master* again. I identified with Antoine Doinel, being roughly the same age as Jean-Pierre Léaud in the film, even though my upbringing couldn't have been more different.

The 400 Blows
23 × 33 in (59 × 84 cm)

UN FILM DE FRANÇOIS TRUFFAUT

Directed by FRANÇOIS TRUFFAUT
Written by FRANÇOIS TRUFFAUT MARCEL MOUSSY
Starring JEAN-PIERRE LÉAUD ALBERT RÉMY CLAIRE MAURIER
Music by JEAN CONSTANTIN
Cinematography HENRI DECAË

INFLUENCES: Akira Kurosawa, Woody Allen, Seijun Suzuki, Masaki Kobayashi, Jacques Tati, Werner Herzog, Sergio Leone, David Lean, Jack Cardiff, Gordon Willis, Henri Matisse, Pablo Picasso, Alberto Giacometti, Goseki Kojima, and Tetsuo Hara. Plus film posters and cover art from any generation.

FAVORITE FILM / GENRE: I love Japanese films, regardless of the genre or time period. There are too many to list here, but anything with Tatsuya Nakadai or Bunta Sugawara tops my list.

FIRST FILM: My mother took me to the movie theater to see Walt Disney's *The Jungle Book*. At home it was either *High Noon* or the Marx Brothers' *A Night at the Opera*. Both were watched on special occasions, way past my bedtime.

PREFERRED MEDIUM: Chinese ink. I love its instant, decisive marks and organic lines. The washes give you a range of depth similar to watercolors. I always travel with a little Chinese ink set.

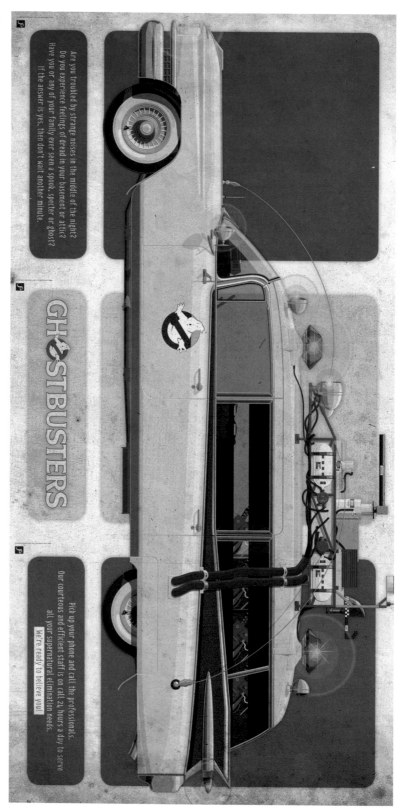

Jakob Vig Stærmose

LOCATION Odense / Denmark

SITE Society6.com/staermose

Ghostbusters
24 × 36 in (61 × 91 cm) / triptych set

Are you troubled by strange noises in the middle of the night?
Do you experience feelings of dread in your basement or attic?
Have you or any of your family ever seen a spook, specter or ghost?
If the answer is yes, then don't wait another minute.

GHOSTBUSTERS

Pick up your phone and call the professionals.
Our courteous and efficient staff is on call 24 hours a day to serve
all your supernatural elimination needs.
We're ready to believe you!

BEHIND THE POSTERS: I've always been drawing. One of my earliest memories is drawing in my bedroom. My grandfather was a sign painter and my father worked with illustrations in advertising. I guess it was only natural that I would hold a pencil in my tiny hands. Later I was formally educated as a graphic designer. That said, it wasn't until my mid-thirties that I started creating illustrations professionally. An old high school friend had some illustration needs, and at that point I realized that illustrations were much more fun than what I had been doing.

A poster set by Mondo helped me find my path. It was a triptych set of the DeLorean time machine from *Back to the Future*. It was sold out, but I initially thought, "I can do that!" I couldn't. I had to learn how to draw vehicles, not necessarily like they did at Mondo, but how I saw them. Having a hobby where I built model kits led me to begin the drawings as technical blueprints. Ecto-1 (from *Ghostbusters*), shown here, was my second vehicle. I loved creating the Ecto-1, not only because of *Ghostbusters* (it's one of my favorite comedies), but also because it is based on a real car, a 1959 Cadillac Miller-Meteor ambulance. I really wanted to show all the little gadgets on top of the car, as well as what was stored inside. *Blade Runner* is in my top five favorite films of all time. We didn't have easy access to video rental where I grew up in the '80s, so I didn't see the film until I was fourteen or fifteen. So the 995 police car from *Blade Runner* was a must for me.

Blade Runner
24 × 36 in (61 × 91 cm) / triptych set

INFLUENCES: I watched a lot of Disney movies as a kid, especially *The Rescuers*. Later I realized that I typically use colored lines for drawings instead of black lines, just like they did for Miss Bianca in that movie. Another influence is Jim Henson's Muppets and their use of bright colors. As an adult I draw a lot of inspiration from Leiji Matsumoto.

FAVORITE FILM / GENRE: Science fiction and fantasy.

PREFERRED MEDIUM: I nearly always use Adobe Illustrator for the final drawing. I use my phone's camera for reference photos when I can, and always sketch freehand, but for the finished product I turn to my laptop. I use a Wacom Intuos digitizer.

CLIENTS: Hero Complex Gallery / US, Tomenosuke / Japan, Geek-Art / France.

ADDITIONAL REMARKS: The biggest reward that I've gained from my artwork is the vast amount of creative people that I have met. I am humbled that so many have contacted me to purchase my drawings.

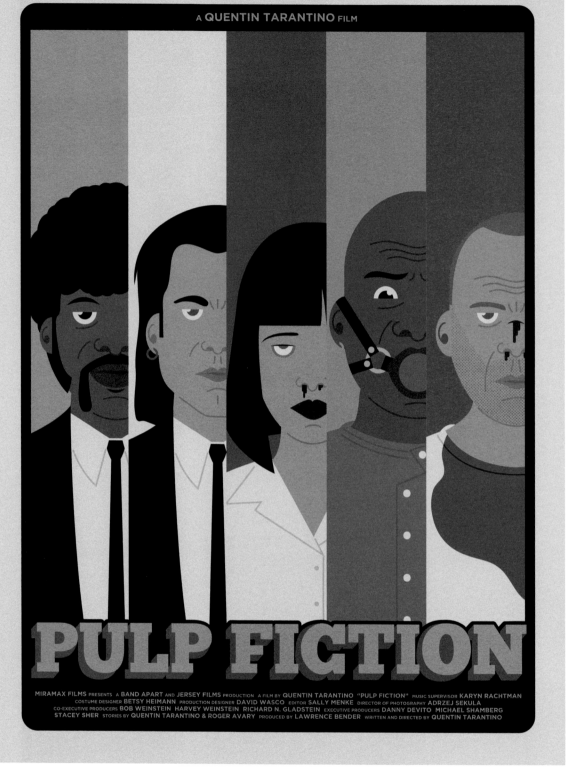

BEHIND THE POSTERS: The *Pulp Fiction* poster is part of an ongoing project called "Pop Culture Series," while the *Super 8* poster was a limited edition screen print for Gallery 1988s J. J. Abrams art show.

INFLUENCES: I am mainly influenced by vintage / retro graphic design. Everything from packaging design, colors, layouts, typography—I'm into all of it. There's something about the simple aesthetic that just mesmerizes me.

FAVORITE FILM / GENRE: If I had to go with a single genre, it would probably be horror. I was desensitized at an early age and grew up watching all of the '80s and '90s R-rated horror movies. So they all stuck with me. It's fun to go back and watch some of those old horror films. Now that I'm older I have a totally new view on them and can appreciate them more. My favorite movie of all time? *Ghostbusters*, hands down.

IT ARRIVES

SUPER 8

FROM WRITER/DIRECTOR
J.J. ABRAMS
AND PRODUCER
STEVEN SPIELBERG

PARAMOUNT PICTURES PRESENTS AN AMBLIN ENTERTAINMENT / BAD ROBOT PRODUCTION "SUPER 8"
VISUAL EFFECTS BY INDUSTRIAL LIGHT & MAGIC VISUAL EFFECTS PRODUCER CHANTAL FEGHALI MUSIC BY MICHAEL GIACCHINO COSTUME DESIGNER HA NGUYEN
EDITED BY MARY JO MARKEY A.C.E. MARYANN BRANDON A.C.E. PRODUCTION DESIGNER MARTIN WHIST DIRECTOR OF PHOTOGRAPHY LARRY FONG EXECUTIVE PRODUCER GUY RIEDEL
PRODUCED BY STEVEN SPIELBERG J.J. ABRAMS BRYAN BURK WRITTEN AND DIRECTED BY J.J. ABRAMS

Artwork by Andrew Heath · www.andrew-heath.com

AMBLIN
ENTERTAINMENT

PREFERRED MEDIUM: Although I can draw, I mainly work digitally in Adobe Illustrator. Once I began to work on a computer, I got lazy and hardly touched a pencil to paper anymore. When printing, I do everything digital. However, if something limited-edition comes up, I screen print.

CLIENTS: Looney Labs, Storey Publishing, The Vendy Awards, H&R Block.

Piranha
18 × 24 in (46 × 61 cm)

ALIAS / DESIGN FIRM	QFSChris of Quiltface Studios
LOCATION	Philadelphia, Pennsylvania / US
SITE	Quiltfacestudios.tumblr.com + Quiltfacestudios.storenvy.com

BEHIND THE POSTERS: *Piranha* contains every ingredient that makes up the perfect B-movie. I watched it repeatedly as a kid, so when I had the chance to tackle it in print form there was no way I could pass it up. *Event Horizon* is a film that taps into the deepest, darkest places in your mind and brings your worst fears to life. The concept for the print was born from a nightmare that I had no idea existed in my psyche until it was brought to life on paper.

RECENT PROJECTS: New concepts for *Halloween III* and *The Texas Chainsaw Massacre*, gallery theme shows, and Poster Posse projects. Favorite past projects would have to be *Godzilla* and a gig poster for *Goblin*—bucket list projects now crossed off.

PINCH ME MOMENT: Clive Barker posting my *Nightbreed* print on his personal Instagram was easily the most flattering experience. Horror convention fans show me a lot of love every time I have a booth. It's humbling when they seek me out to tell me in person how much they like my work.

Event Horizon
18 × 24 in (46 × 61 cm)

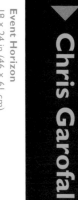

ALIAS / DESIGN FIRM	LOCATION	SITE
QFSChris of Quiltface Studios	Philadelphia, Pennsylvania / US	Quiltfacestudios.tumblr.com + Quiltfacestudios.storenvy.com

IS THE FILM INDUSTRY COMING ALONG? It seems that the tide is shifting more toward commissioning traditional artists, which I really hope continues and develops. Nowadays, fans want a more personal, collectible, and attractive product, and artists like us are just the ones for the job. I'd love to see things go back to the old VHS tape look, everything custom illustrated and unique.

CLIENTS: The Colonial Theatre, Bottleneck Gallery, Hero Complex Gallery, Goblin, Days of the Dead Convention, Paramount, Living Dead Dolls.
ADDITIONAL REMARKS: "Always stay true to the idea." —David Lynch

Graham Erwin

Charlie and the Chocolate Factory
24 × 36 in (61 × 91 cm)
A DzXtinKt Originals release

DESIGN FIRM	Delicious Design League
LOCATION	Columbus, Ohio / US
SITE	Grahamerwin.com

BEHIND THE POSTERS: *Charlie and the Chocolate* factory was commissioned by Dzxtinkt Originals. When they approached me about creating a poster for Roald Dahl's original book [vs. the film], I was extremely excited, because this twist allowed me more creative liberty. Creating posters for popular films can be fun, but also restrictive because of dealing with actor's likenesses. For this reason I chose to make the factory the main focus of the illustration, and took advantage of the large print format by adding as many little details as possible. This is an image that needs to be seen in person to be appreciated.

The Life Aquatic poster was created in 2012 for a Gallery 1998 group show "Post No Bills," which paid tribute to Bill Murray. After some brainstorming I decided to use *The Life Aquatic* as inspiration due to Wes Anderson's bright and whimsical visuals in the movie. The process was a blast. I ended up watching the film over and over on my laptop, filling up pages of notes on all the little "easter eggs" that I could hide in the poster details. This was also one of the main images that caught Mondo's eye when they first approached about working with them, which was obviously a game changer in my career.

The Life Aquatic with Steve Zissou
16 × 24 in (41 × 61 cm)

INFLUENCES: In my early years, much of my influence came from the flattened perspectives of 16-bit video games, plus graffiti and murals that I would see around town. At a young age this imagery really stuck with me, and when working on an illustration I always want to evoke the same emotions that I felt as a kid looking at art. Currently I am inspired by my friends and contemporaries in the poster world. Outside of the visual arts, I am obsessed with music, mainly the darker, experimental variety.

FAVORITE FILM / GENRE: Horror films all the way.
FIRST FILM: One of the first films that stuck with me was *Alien*. The chest-burster scene left an indelible impression on my young mind.
PREFERRED MEDIUM: Adobe Illustrator with a bit of retouching in Photoshop.
CLIENTS: Mondo, *Wired*, ESPN, NPR, Grovemade, Sony, Gallery 1988, and more.

National Lampoon's Christmas Vacation
18 × 24 in (46 × 61 cm)

DESIGN FIRM PAIDesign (Paul Ainsworth Illustration & Design)
LOCATION Toronto, Ontario / Canada
SITE Paidesign.net

BEHIND THE POSTERS: *Christmas Vacation* was made for a group gallery show called "Alternate Ending" in Brooklyn, New York, at Bottleneck Gallery. This was a "what if" show where artists were asked to depict a different ending for one of their favorite films. I think there would have been some comedy gold in seeing Clark and Cousin Eddie go to jail. Hell, it could be a great start to a new film on its own.

I was also asked to participate in Hero Complex's show "Kings of Cult: An Art Tribute to Roger Corman and Joe Dante." I chose *The 'Burbs*, one of my favorite films. I originally wanted to create an "ode to a famous ginger" and have Hanz be the big visual winner in the piece, but then I thought that this would only be funny or interesting to me (a fellow

ginger). So, I went back to the drawing board. I feel bad about leaving out Corey Feldman, but the scene I wanted to depict didn't need him. Sales of this piece and the two variant versions sold out and got a lot of hype. What made me happy was seeing Dick Miller sign someone's poster. Yes, "that guy," also known as "Garbageman #1" on IMDB!

INFLUENCES: To name a few poster artists that have influenced my work, Gary Pullin, Jason Edmiston, and Justin Erickson are not only amazing talents, but really down-to-earth folks. Salvador Anguiano, Matt Tobin, Chris Garofalo, Orlando Arocena, and a whole whack more have made a great impression on me personally and artistically.

Paul Ainsworth

The 'Burbs
18 × 24 in (46 × 61 cm)

DESIGN FIRM PAIDesign (Paul Ainsworth Illustration & Design)

LOCATION Toronto, Ontario / Canada

SITE Paidesign.net

I grew up reading comics and it led me to becoming an artist, so guys like Todd McFarlane, Greg Capullo, Jae Lee, Steven Hughes, Stephen Platt, and Dale Keown all had some deep hooks in my passion for art. Music has also influenced my art. In high school, I stayed at home while others went out and partied. Being a Gen-Xer, I'd throw on some Smashing Pumpkins, Nine Inch Nails, or some Pearl Jam and find a groove to keep drawing.

FAVORITE FILM / GENRE: I have a collection of over 300 films. I'm a sucker for retro '80s flicks like *Pee-Wee's Big Adventure* and *Ghostbusters*, but also love flicks like *The Hunt for Red October*, so I'm not stuck on a particular genre. I'm also a fan of superhero movies, as well as cult films like *The Big Lebowski*. If I can be honest, I'm also a closet *Harry Potter* fan. If I were to nail down one film that I could watch over and over, it's *The Life Aquatic*.

PREFERRED MEDIUM: Hand-drawn images, followed by Adobe Illustrator.

CLIENTS: WWE, Tony Hawk Clothing, Warner Music Group, AMC, and the National Hockey League. Plus galleries including Hero Complex, Bottleneck, Spoke Art Gallery, LTD, and Gauntlet.

ADDITIONAL REMARKS: Although relatively new to the scene, I've made a ton of friends from all over the globe. I've also been inspired by the artistic community, as well as by fans and the support that comes along with it. Regardless of success, art brings us together in a discussion. It doesn't have to be a "dog eat dog" world, especially when we're talking about creativity. You can create all you want, but if you have no one to show it to, what's the point?

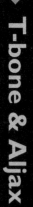

Planes, Trains and Automobiles
19 × 25 in (48 × 64 cm)
A Blunt Graffix release

DESIGNERS Allen Jackson & Tony Jackson

LOCATION Reading, Pennsylvania / US

SITE Tbonealjax.com

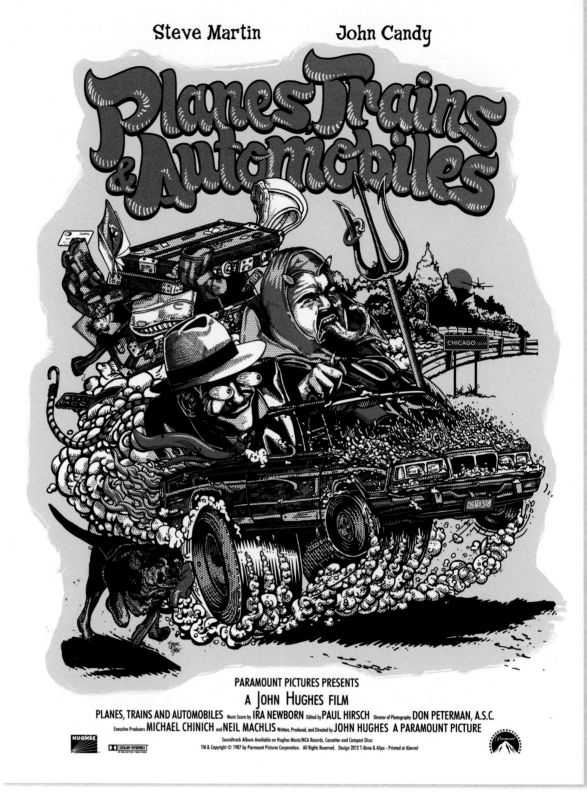

BEHIND THE POSTERS: "Contrast makes good art." —Tom Volpicelli / The Mastering House

This is a phrase that sticks with us when we make pop culture prints. *Planes, Trains, and Automobiles* was created for a show called "Blunt Funk." Matt Dye from Blunt Graffix coordinated the show, which celebrated the work of Kustom Kulture originator Ed ("Big Daddy") Roth. The idea was to choose a movie and combine it with the big wheels, smoke plumes, popped eyeballs, and other bad-ass elements found in Ed's work. So we, along with a handful of other gig poster artists, came up with ideas ranging from *Easy Rider* to *Star Wars*. The contrast here is simple: take a family-friendly comedy with two superstar comedy actors that are traveling home for Thanksgiving dinner and mix it with this amazing underground custom car art style.

Planes, Trains and Automobiles is one of those films that never received handmade poster attention, so we jumped on it. The details were crucial in this one, and we pored over the film at least ten times, taking notes on how to manipulate every detail: the snowy, burned up Lincoln Town and Country (the car is on fire so that there could be a source for the excess smoke plumes); the dog from Owens truck with the glove running alongside the car; Del's trunk overflowing with his pajamas, pillow and shower curtain rings; and Neil Page's necktie that re-creates the look of the fink tongue dangling out of the car. Del's steering wheel is even bent forward.

"Nouveau Riche Oblige." *Clue* was by far one of our favorite comedies growing up. This is one of those films that we can recite front to back from memory. The cast, wit, and timing are all perfection. This print is a big departure from the way that we normally make our posters, in that it

142

DESIGNERS	Allen Jackson & Tony Jackson
LOCATION	Reading, Pennsylvania / US
SITE	Tbonealjax.com

gives nothing about the movie away. We really wanted to bring out what is fundamentally frightening about the idea of going to a spooky mansion laced with government secrets, blackmail, and murder. We place the viewer of this poster in the position of one of the murderees (the telegram girl, the cop) who is greeted at the door by a group of stone-faced potential killers with weapons in tow. Tim Curry gets away with his devilish smirk for obvious reasons. We normally don't do variants, but in this case we felt that a mirrored print really helped to drive this concept home.

INFLUENCES: David Lynch, Quentin Tarantino, Stanley Kubrick, the Coen brothers, Spike Jonze, too many comic book artists to list, Robert Crumb, Paolo Serpieri, Mary Blair, Chuck Jones, Will Vinton, Milt Kahl, Jim Henson, Richard Donner, Jim Davis, Bill Watterson, Gary Baseman, and Art Spiegelman.

FAVORITE FILM / GENRE: Comedies and horror movies.
PREFERRED MEDIUM: Pen and ink, silkscreen.
CLIENTS: We've created a ton of gig posters (for Queens of the Stone Age, Ween, Chromeo, My Morning Jacket, Lotus, The National, Death Cab for Cutie, Primus, Elvis Costello, Sufjan Stevens, Bon Iver, Elton John . . . the list goes on). Plus prints for comedians (Jim Gaffigan, Donald Gover, Conan O'Brien), album covers (VHS or Beta, American Babies, Eagle and the Worm, Brothers Past). We've recently been creating pop culture prints with various galleries.

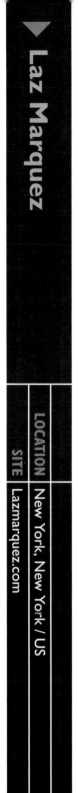

The Birds
18 × 27 in (46 × 69 cm)

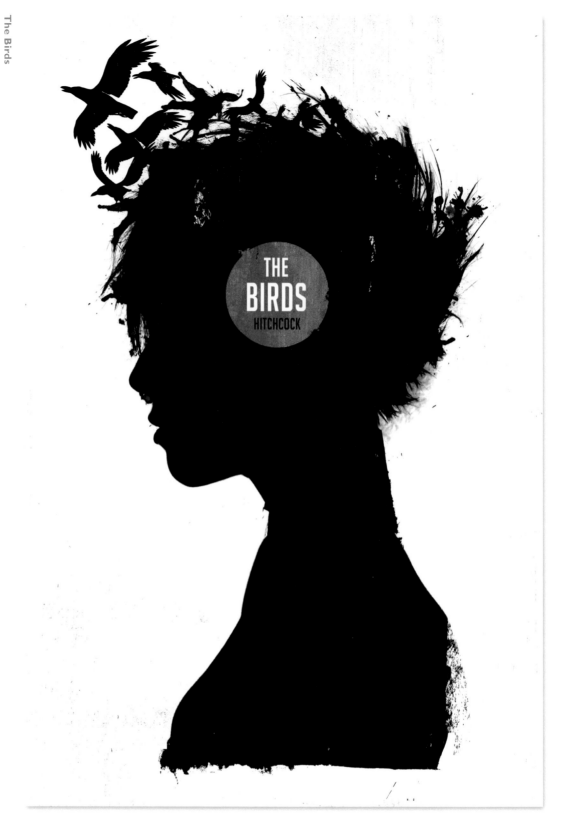

THE
BIRDS
HITCHCOCK

BEHIND THE POSTERS: Having grown up with film, specifically the horror and thriller genres, I was compelled to pay tribute to "The Master of Suspense" himself, Alfred Hitchcock. As an artist, I have always been drawn to and inspired by stories about the people and struggles in Hitchcock's work. I wanted to evoke the anxiety and suspense his direction brought to life in a simple, fresh, and painterly way that left the viewer feeling there is much more mystery to the story.

INFLUENCES: Alfred Hitchcock, Chip Kidd, Frida Kahlo, and Egon Schiele.
FAVORITE FILM / GENRE: Horror, science fiction, and mystery.

Laz Marquez

LOCATION New York, New York / US

SITE Lazmarquez.com

FIRST FILM: *Aliens* and *Jurassic Park* created a universe that I truly believed in as a child, with strong characters that fought the odds and drove the films forward.

PREFERRED MEDIUM: I am a digital and fine art hybrid.

LOCATION Astoria, New York / US

SITE Stevedressler.com

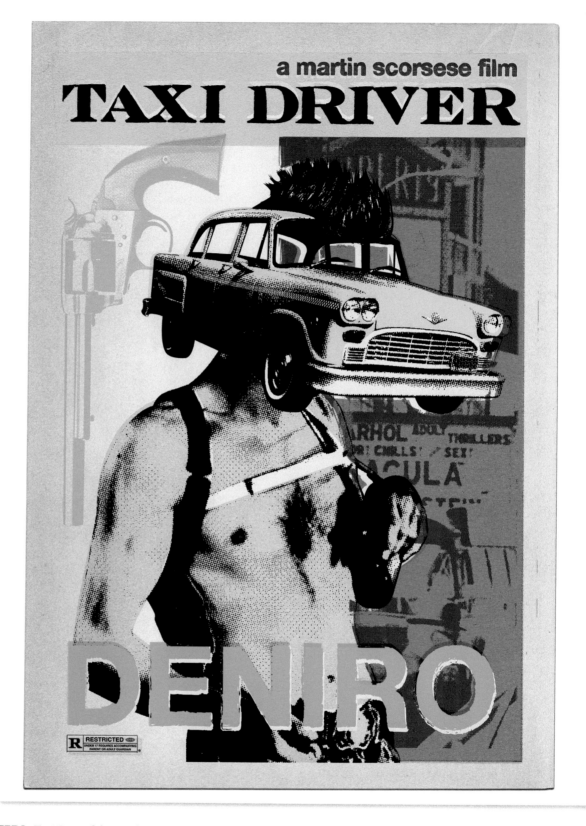

BEHIND THE POSTERS: *Taxi Driver* [also used as a basis for the *Alternative Movie Posters* volume one book cover.] This was the first film that I can remember seeing that wasn't a movie—it was a *film*. It dealt with adult themes in a mature and crafted manner. The artisanship showed itself in all of the elements that go into a film. The acting was intense. The cinematography was gritty. Growing up in Queens, it was my first view of life over the bridge in Manhattan. The stories about Forty-second Street were true! This film allowed me to view movies with a more discerning and grown-up point of view. I was probably too young when I first saw it, but I was able to navigate and comprehend what was going on.

Visually, I think that I've had the mohawk taxicab head in my brain for almost fifteen years. It was something that popped in my head when I

watched the film again in my early twenties. It took me a while to be able to pull that from my brain and get it on a page.

Little Shop. The 1986 version of *Little Shop of Horrors* is so visually captivating that it is hard to ignore. It's a musical fairy tale come to life in vibrant color. Rick Moranis is the perfect everyman, singing his heart out against love and space monsters. I have loved everything Moranis has ever done, back to the times of SCTV when my family would gather around and laugh together. I remember seeing the movie in the theater during Christmastime. One image that stuck with me was Moranis' red jacket, like James Dean. It was a joke that I somehow understood and felt smart for catching it. And the Maxwell House coffee can that housed Audrey II was so graphically iconic. It probably planted a seed, so to speak, for my love of vintage packaging. It really felt like a comic book movie. Scenes would end

Little Shop of Horrors
12 × 9 in (30 × 23 cm)

Steve Dressler

LOCATION	Astoria, New York / US
SITE	Stevedressler.com

SUDDENLY...

DRESSLER

with wipes and/or scenery being pulled away. A true classic that I always come back to.

In terms of the book cover for *Alternative Movie Posters II*, the author and I both ended up naming one of our most beloved childhood icons, Pee-Wee Herman. I could preach the glory of Paul Reubens' creation forever. His visual taste was the perfect mix of 1980s pop and retro kitsch. I watched his first HBO special as a young kid, and knew it word-for-word upon repeated viewings. When *Pee-Wee's Big Adventure* came out, it was like ninety minutes of pure rock candy. Colorful and funny with a little bit of edge. Tim Burton was an instant visual master and hung the perfect frame around Pee-Wee's universe. The plotline was so straightforward (a boy who wants his bike back), but the film was incredibly written and masterfully visualized. This is my favorite film. Period.

INFLUENCES: Warhol, Lichtenstein, Haring, Duchamp, cereal boxes, my brother's comic collection, graffiti.
FAVORITE FILM / GENRE: Comedies and documentaries.
FIRST FILM: *The Jerk*.
PREFERRED MEDIUM: Digital or painting (...but I can't choose one over the other).
CLIENTS: *This American Life*, Conan, VH1, Upright Citizens Brigade.

Groundhog Day
17 × 24 in (42 × 60 cm)

DESIGN FIRM | Kindred Studio

LOCATION | Sydney, New South Wales / Australia

SITE | Kindredstudio.net

BEHIND THE POSTERS: With *Groundhog Day*, I had recently re-watched the (genius) film. I wanted to bring a different approach to what I had typically seen in poster artwork (i.e., the alarm clock/5:59 a.m. theme). I had a huge grin on my face the whole time I was working on the image seen here.

Boogie Nights was created for *Little White Lies* magazine's 50th issue. As a big Paul Thomas Anderson fan, I was really pleased to work with this firm, and again, I wanted to approach it from an unexpected angle. So I envisioned how an adult film newspaper may have interpreted Dirk Diggler's fall from grace at the time.

DESIGN FIRM	Kindred Studio
LOCATION	Sydney, New South Wales / Australia
SITE	Kindredstudio.net

INFLUENCES: Art Chantry, Istvan Orosz, Sean Tejaratchi, Michael Leon, Peter Saville, Push Pin Graphic, Wallace Wood, Dave Gibbons, Haruki Murakami, Warhol, Michel Gondry, David Lynch and a ton of anonymous mid-century commercial illustrators.

FAVORITE FILM / GENRE: Film = *Chopper*. Genre = anything dark with a sense of humor.

FIRST FILM: *The Empire Strikes Back*.
PREFERRED MEDIUM: Pen, ink, silkscreen.
CLIENTS: *Little White Lies*, *GQ*, *Wired*, ESPN, Penguin, Random House, Ride Snowboards, Mr. Black.

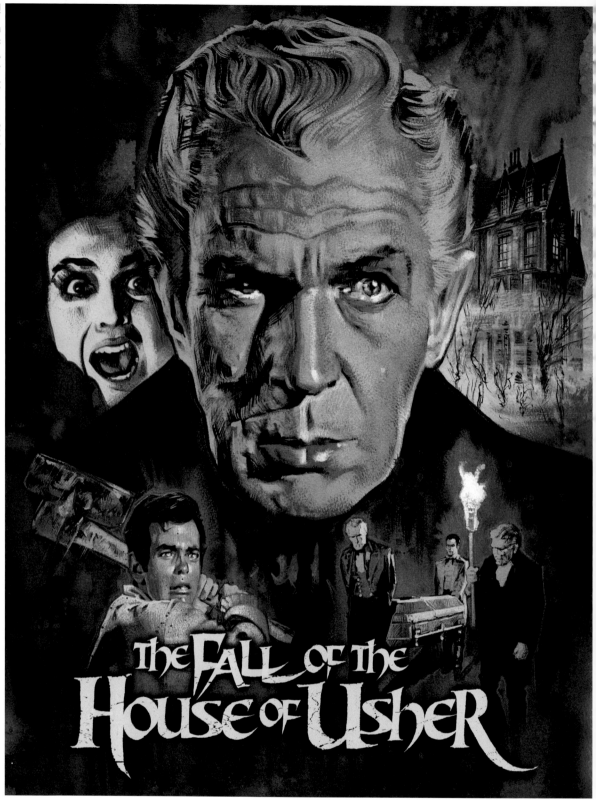

BEHIND THE POSTERS: Both *The Fall of the House of Usher* and *Super Bitch* are Blu-ray covers commissioned by Arrow Films in the UK. *The Fall of the House of Usher* was a film that I recall seeing on late night television in my early teens. I was fascinated by the strange hybrid setting that was at once European and yet so Californian. The sound design and lighting worked wonderfully on my cheap monochrome, portable television set. Only years later did I finally get the full impact of the lurid colors that exploded over every scene—weirdly psychedelic and intoxicating. Of course, the Vincent Price performance is central to the film and I wanted to capture his tortured, theatrical face that makes it so watchable. *The House* itself was always the metaphor for the crumbling sanity and corruption of an inbred bloodline, and the poster flanks the face of Roderick alongside the deranged features of

Madeline. The lower elements are intended to convey narrative content, the promise of action, and the "live" burial within the bowels of the building. All of these trap Vincent's face, just as he is trapped within his own madness. Although the film has its own palettes, I used the colors I had imagined while watching the film all those years ago on my little black-and-white set: purples for decadence and greens for mold and corruption. All of this is painted with tortured textures and splashes to evoke decay.

Unfamiliar with *Super Bitch*, I watched a copy of the film to get a feel for the narrative and visual hooks. Clearly Stephanie Beacham was going to be the focal point, and the inclusion of Ivan Rassimov was a client requirement. Enjoying the film and dizzied by the genre blend, I felt that my best approach involved creating a pastiche of erotic, thriller, euro-crime using composition and a color palette that was firmly rooted in the era in which the film was made (1973). I wanted to accentuate the title with part of the image overlapping, the

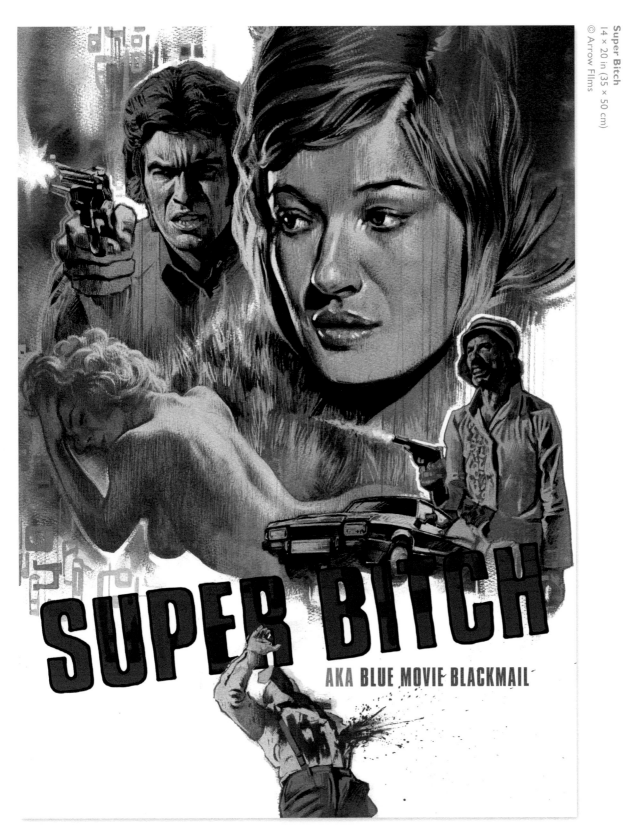

Graham Humphreys

LOCATION	London / UK
SITE	Grahamhumphreys.com

gunshot victim tumbling backwards, as if the name alone would have killed him! Also, the featured male characters look desperate as they fire almost aimlessly in the air, while Stephanie Beacham looks completely in control despite the deceptively passive nudity.

Rather than "bitch" in the derogatory sense, I wanted to make this a poster for a film that celebrated the sort of strong female that aggressive men find so threatening. The men are out-smarted, the woman out-trumps the phallic guns!

INFLUENCES: My work owes a great debt to the film poster illustration work of Struzan, Peak, and all of the many artists that I never knew the names of. My color palettes were originally influenced by the Aurora monster kit collection, then refined by trips overseas and seeing the different approaches to color that other cultures use. Beyond the visual influence I have found music a massive influence on my work, particularly the early UK punk scene and the

ripples that it created (The Cramps, The Gun Club, Siouxsie and the Banshees).
FAVORITE FILM / GENRE: From 1960s television—*Dr. Who*, *Lost in Space*, *The Munsters*, *The Addams Family*, the work of Poe and Lovecraft, and the acknowledged horror classics that spawned the Universal Monsters and Hammer Horror. I still enjoy odd and transgressive ideas, and horror is possibly the best medium for understanding the human fear of "other," be it race, sex, religious, or political.
PREFERRED MEDIUM: Gouache (a water-based medium) is my preference for painting. I find it versatile and it delivers the results that I seek.
CLIENTS: The campaigns for *The Evil Dead* and *A Nightmare On Elm Street*, for UK's Palace Pictures, defined my career and the legacy of the early work still resonates for my current clients (Arrow, of course, among them).

Jonathan Burton

LOCATION Bordeaux / France

SITE Jonathanburton.net

20,000 Leagues Under the Sea
24 x 36 in (61 x 91 cm)

BEHIND THE POSTERS: Nautilus Art Prints asked me to work with them on a screen print for their "European Culture" collection. I thought it was a great idea to concentrate on this rich, historical topic, and with *20,000 Leagues Under the Sea* being so iconic, I suggested it as a print. They were very keen on the idea. This was my first screen print, and with Jack and Laurent Durieux acting as art directors, the process was a great learning experience.

The *Argo* illustration was commissioned by BAFTA (British Academy of Film and Television Arts) for one of their Best Film nominations in 2013. I illustrated five posters in total, with the other nominees being *Les Misérables*, *Life of Pi*, *Lincoln*, and *Zero Dark Thirty*. There was an extremely short

deadline, as the awards evening comes soon after the nominations; I had ten days to produce artwork for five posters. It was exhausting, but also liberating.
INFLUENCES: I love the look of Victorian fashion plates, but also of illustrators of the period like J. J. Grandville, Alphonse de Neuville, and Felicien Rops. Absurdity is a big influence, too, so Monty Python, Spike Milligan, Vic Reeves, and Bob Mortimer all tickle my ribs, along with "nonsense" illustrator Edward Lear. Another influence is the music that I listen to when working on a piece. I try to match the music to the artwork. It sets the mood and makes the designs click into place. Film soundtracks are always helpful; some of my favorite composers are Alexandre Desplat and Jonny Greenwood.

152

FAVORITE FILM / GENRE: I like psychological horror, and *The Haunting*, by Robert Wise, is the best of the genre. It's unusual in that it shows us very little (it's all about suggestion). The unusual camera angles, moody lighting, and slow build of suspense make it very unsettling.

FIRST FILM: My first film at the cinema was *Snow White and the Seven Dwarfs*. At the time, Disney re-released it every seven years, and I saw it with my dad. It's an innocent story, but at the same time I found it creepy. I still love the film, and have watched it many times with my kids. It's beautifully designed by another of my illustration heroes, Gustaf Tenggren.

PREFERRED MEDIUM: Pencil and digital.

CLIENTS: Book publishers include the Folio Society, Penguin Books, Milan Editions, Random House, and Vintage. I have many editorial clients including *The New York Times*, *The Boston Globe*, *New Scientist*, *The Telegraph*, and *The Times*. Others clients of note include BAFTA, The Royal Mail, Care for the Wild, Nautilus Art Prints, and Mondo.

Matt Ryan Tobin

Halloween
(actual title = *Death Has Come to Your Little Town*)
36 × 24 in (91 × 61 cm)

LOCATION Hamilton, Ontario / Canada

SITE Worksofmattryan.com

BEHIND THE POSTERS: For *Death Has Come to Your Little Town* [based on *Halloween*], I wanted to create a film poster with a minimalist art deco vibe. Plus, of course, a hint of menace (the unforeseen, looming style of danger from the film). I also wanted to feature Laurie at the helm for a change. She's an important character to the film, and to be honest, the entire horror genre.

We'll Be Right Back was created for the Hero Complex Gallery show "Kings of Cult: An Art Tribute to Roger Corman and Joe Dante" and was inspired by *Gremlins 2: The New Batch*. The cameos and pop culture references that riddle this film are great. I love how they refer to plot holes from the first film, especially involving the metamorphosis of the Mogwai themselves. I wanted to capture the craziness of these creatures taking over the Clamp building, as well as feature some of the iconic Gremlins from the sequel.

FAVORITE FILM / GENRE: *Halloween* is a favorite, plus '70s to early '90s horror. If a film has Pauly Shore in it or features the word "dude" a lot, then I probably love it.

154

▼ Matt Ryan Tobin

Gremlins 2: The New Batch
(actual title = *We'll Be Right Back*)
24 × 18 in (61 × 46 cm)

| LOCATION | Hamilton, Ontario / Canada |
| SITE | Worksofmattryan.com |

FIRST FILM: *Bill & Ted's Excellent Adventure.* That was my "babysitter" growing up. If Mom wanted me out of her hair, she'd pop in the VHS and I was glued to the screen. Although I'm now far more favorable to *Bill & Ted's Bogus Journey,* which is my all-time favorite film.

PREFERRED MEDIUM: I sometimes use pencil and inks, but mostly digital illustration (Wacom and Photoshop) and screen printing. With screen printing, it's real. It has texture. You can feel it. But it also has flaws (it's never quite perfect), and I like that.

CLIENTS: Odd City Entertainment, Fright Rags, Iron Fist, All That Remains, Every Time I Die, and Cancer Bats, to name a few.

ADDITIONAL REMARKS: I'm grateful for what I have been able to create thus far, and for the amazing artists and people who I have met along the way. "Art should comfort the disturbed and disturb the comfortable." —Cesar A. Cruz

CENTURIES
OF PASSION
PENT UP IN HIS
SAVAGE HEART!

BEHIND THE POSTERS: *Creature from the Black Lagoon* has always been one of my favorite Universal Monsters, and I really wanted to do a poster that was different from others out there. I focused on one of my favorite moments from the movie, when the creature tried to touch Julie Adams' feet while she was swimming. From a human perspective this was terrifying, but from the creature's angle, he was more curious and a little sad because of his lonely existence.

Temple of Doom was the first of the *Indiana Jones* movies that I watched. I feel that *Doom* is very underrated and wanted to do a fun B-movie poster for it, reflecting the film's attitude and color palette. Instead of painting it traditionally, I used pen and ink wash to draw the subjects, and then applied color digitally to give it a simpler look.

Blain Hefner

LOCATION	San Marcos, Texas / US
SITE	Hefnatron.com

INFLUENCES: There are so many. I am constantly being inspired by different artists. My core influences are Steven Spielberg; painters Drew Struzan, Reynold Brown and Jason Edmiston; and comic artists Darwyn Cooke, Jack Kirby, and Al Williamson.

FAVORITE FILM / GENRE: *Raiders of the Lost Ark* is my favorite film, as it has the perfect balance of drama, action, and comedy. However, I'm usually drawn to science fiction more than anything. A big chunk of the films that influence my work come from the '80s.

FIRST FILM: *E.T.* Even though I was only four, I was more engaged by the puppetry and special effects than the emotional component of the story. When E.T. died and people in the theater were sobbing, I wanted to tell them it was okay, because he was only a puppet.

Cronos
11 × 17 in (28 × 43 cm) / printed on wood

DESIGN FIRM Chogrin Inc.
LOCATION Guayaquil / Ecuador
SITE Chogrin.com

BEHIND THE POSTERS: Guillermo del Toro has been a huge inspiration in the last decade. Since watching *Blade 2* (2002), I've collected and watched all of his films. From DVD commentaries, interviews, and art books, his artistic vision and passion are evident. I therefore illustrated what I call his personal trilogy: *Cronos* [above left], *The Devil's Backbone*, and *Pan's Labyrinth* [above right]. I believe these films represent del Toro's voice in its purest form. They contain various color layers, symbols, and eye protein for any type of artist to dissect and feast on. These pieces were originally created for an art gallery I curated back in 2013 called "Into the Labyrinth and Mind of Guillermo del Toro." You can read more about it here: http://gdtart.blogspot.com/p/about.html.

RECENT PROJECTS: This year I curated two of my dream-come-true art gallery shows. In the first, I worked with one of my art heroes, Mike Mignola, for the official *Hellboy* 20th anniversary art show. The show was a big success and was celebrated with a cake in the form of a giant stack of pancakes! The second was working with Frank Caruso and King Features Syndicate for the official *Popeye the Sailor* 85th anniversary art show. I dedicated this show to my grandfather, Manuel Game Peña, an Ecuadorian marine, who was a real life Popeye and hero to me growing up.

Pan's Labyrinth
11 × 17 in (28 × 43 cm) / printed on wood

CHOGRIN

DESIGN FIRM	Chogrin Inc.
LOCATION	Guayaquil / Ecuador
SITE	Chogrin.com

チョグリン

PINCH ME MOMENT: One of my favorite moments this year was receiving a message from John Bell, the art director of *Jurassic Park*, saying that he really liked my *Dino-DNA* illustration print that was inspired by his Barbasol / Dino-DNA Cryocan Cannister from the movie. More here: http://chogrin.bigcartel.com/product/dino-dna-print.

IS THE FILM INDUSTRY COMING ALONG? I am noticing that artists with strong art chops and web presence are getting featured a lot more to create official movie posters or limited edition prints. You no longer have to be part of Mondo to get your work featured as part of an official movie campaign. Great art is being seen and speaking for itself. I think that this is a result of a growing appreciation for movie art and pop culture; people are tired of flashy, forgettable Photoshopped posters.

CLIENTS: King Features Syndicate, Cartoon Network, Deltorofilms.com.
ADDITIONAL REMARKS: Since I am featuring my del Toro pieces in this book, I thought I'd share that I am curating and creating new artwork for another Guillermo del Toro art show. The show will feature over 100 artists from around the world paying tribute to his films.

Isac Anatol-Nathan

The Bicycle Thief
24 × 18 in (61 × 46 cm)
A FAMP Art release

ALIAS	XUL1349
LOCATION	Bucharest / Romania
SITE	Xul1349.com

BEHIND THE POSTERS: From the moment that Alex of FAMP Art (New York) approached me with the idea of making a poster for *The Bicycle Thief,* we knew that we had to find an angle that would perfectly reflect the story's emotional turmoil. The solution was to minimize Ricci's role as a character and instead focus on him as part of the universe in which he lives. Fun fact: Ricci actually appears twice in the poster.

INFLUENCES: Everything Gothic and Victorian. From the contemporary art scene I would name the likes of Godmachine (who, without knowing, is the main reason I never gave up art), Joshua Andrew Belanger, Dan Mumford, Vania Zouravliov.
FAVORITE FILM / GENRE: My all-time favorite movie is *Rosemary's Baby*, but anything horror will do.

FIRST FILM: The first movie that I was actually aware of would be *Léon*. At the time I was probably too young to see it, but it had a great impact on me.

PREFERRED MEDIUM: Any medium will do. Most of my work is created digitally now, but I never shy away from pencils, inks, or even oils.

Batman
(actual title = *Broken*)
18 × 24 in (46 × 61 cm)

LOCATION Wales / UK

SITE Godmachine.co.uk

BEHIND THE POSTERS: The Joker piece reminded me of Dale Cooper from *Twin Peaks*, and the Henry Rollins photograph [by punk photographer Ed Colver] on the *Black Flag* album. I liked the idea that the Joker is a splintered character and I even bought four mirrors to smash (trying to replicate the image). Sadly, the only thing I learned is that you can't make mirrors break the way you would like. I am not superstitious, so I'm lucky there.

RECENT PROJECTS: I have been creating more posters than T-shirts recently, which has been exciting. I enjoy the physical contact you have with poster-making compared to T-shirts. With posters I get to see every single one. So, in turn, I feel closer to the work.

PINCH ME MOMENT: I am new to the world of comic cons and fandom in the way that it's now known. I never thought much of having a famous person like my work, and that's mainly because I never knew anyone famous. I have made some amazing friends as an artist, and that's more important to me than fame. That said, I recently had a drink with members of Kyuss—a dream come true, and most of all they were so damn awesome.

ARMY *of* DARKNESS

IS THE FILM INDUSTRY COMING ALONG? The industry seems to be taking notice of the trend. There have always been great artists, but just like the music video scene at the end of the '90s (where video directors were suddenly becoming more famous than the music itself), the film industry is realizing that artists such as Mumford and Stout have fan bases that deserve recognition.

CLIENTS: I primarily work on private commissions.
ADDITIONAL REMARKS: I can't believe I am still doing this for a living. Thank you.

ALIAS	Joebot
LOCATION	Los Angeles, California / US
SITE	jo3bot.com

BEHIND THE POSTERS: These pieces were created for a show at Gallery 1988 in Los Angeles called "A Tribute to Edgar Wright." All of the artwork was themed around his work. Edgar himself showed up for the opening, along with his friends Simon Pegg and Nick Frost [from *Shaun of the Dead*].

INFLUENCES: This is a tough one to sum up because, like most artists, my influences come from so many different sources (movies, music, television, video games, books, other artists, etc.). For this series, though, my two big inspirations were the "Little Golden Books" series and the amazingly wonderful artist Mary Blair.

FAVORITE FILM / GENRE: I love the *Lord of the Rings* and *Star Wars* series. I'm also a huge fan of animation, and my favorite animated film is easily *The Iron Giant*. Marvel films are big for me, too, with *Guardians of the Galaxy* being at the top the list.

Shaun of the Dead
8 × 10 in (20 × 25 cm)

a Little Cornetto Book®

EDGAR WRIGHT's
SHAUN OF THE DEAD™

ALIAS	Joebot
LOCATION	Los Angeles, California / US
SITE	Jo3bot.com

FIRST FILM: My parents started taking me to the theater when I was very young. *E.T.* is the first movie I remember seeing glimpses of.

PREFERRED MEDIUM: I work 100 percent digital now but was trained with more traditional mediums. I loved oil painting, but I have traded in the brushes and canvas for a tablet and digital pen.

CLIENTS: In the past I worked for Warner Bros. on a movie project, and then moved to the video game industry for several years, most notably with Electronic Arts on games like *Dead Space* and *The Sims* as a concept artist. I now work full-time as a gallery/freelance artist. I recently collaborated with Sony Pictures on a special edition Blu-ray re-release for *Superbad*, completed my first children's book *Attack! Boss! Cheat Code! A Gamer's Alphabet*, and also had my first solo show at Gallery 1988. With a lot of my work showing in Hollywood, I've had quite a few well-known actors and directors hang my work in their house. This is always flattering, as most of the time I'm also a huge fan of their work.

BEHIND THE POSTERS: A private poster commission group invited me to join them, and later hired me to create new poster designs for *The Wizard of Oz*, with the twist of splitting the cast of characters into two posters. It was a bit of a surprise, because I hadn't designed any classic film posters at that point. Also, it was a challenge to create two interconnecting posters. I'm glad I took on the project and everyone seemed to love the final result.

INFLUENCES: As a kid, I was always fascinated with *Star Wars*, and then growing up I was influenced by video game-related art (i.e., with the works of *Final Fantasy* artists Yoshitaka Amano and Tetsuya Nomura). Lately I've been loving Martin Ansin's work, and think he's a genius to combine the aesthetics of graphic design with his illustration.

The Wizard of Oz
24 × 36 in (61 × 91 cm)

METRO
GOLDWYN MAYER
presents

in TECHNICOLOR

The
WIZARD
of OZ

JUDY GARLAND · FRANK MORGAN · RAY BOLGER · BERT LAHR
JACK HALEY · BILLIE BURKE · MARGARET HAMILTON
CHARLES GRAPEWIN and the MUNCHKINS

screenplay by: NOEL LANGLEY · FLORENCE RYERSON
and · EDGAR ALLAN WOOLF
based on the book by L. FRANK BAUM · directed by VICTOR FLEMING

▼

Vincent Rhafael Aseo

LOCATION Makati, Manila / Philippines

SITE Vincentaseo.com

FAVORITE FILM / GENRE: Noir, sci-fi, suspense/thriller, crime, and anything George Lucas or Christopher Nolan.
FIRST FILM: *Back to the Future* or *Ghostbusters*.
PREFERRED MEDIUM: Digital, vector graphics.

CLIENTS: *GQ, Advanced Photoshop* magazine (UK).
ADDITIONAL REMARKS: It is truly an honor to be a part of the book. Keep spreading the love for alternative movie posters!

Harijs Grundmanis

Django Unchained
24 × 36 in (61 × 91 cm)

ALIAS	Harry Grundmann
LOCATION	Riga / Latvia
SITE	Harrymovieart.com

Poster Art by Harry Grundmann

BEHIND THE POSTERS: Regarding *Django Unchained*, I am a huge fan of Quentin Tarantino (especially *Django*). After completing the poster, some of the prints were sent to Tarantino himself, and he signed one of them at Cannes 2014. With *The Last Stand*, Kim Jee-woon is my favorite South Korean film director, while Arnold Schwarzenegger is my favorite childhood actor. So, creating a poster for *The Last Stand* was a logical progression for me.

INFLUENCES: Quentin Tarantino, Asian cinema, film noir.

ALIAS	Harry Grundmann
LOCATION	Riga / Latvia
SITE	Harrymovieart.com

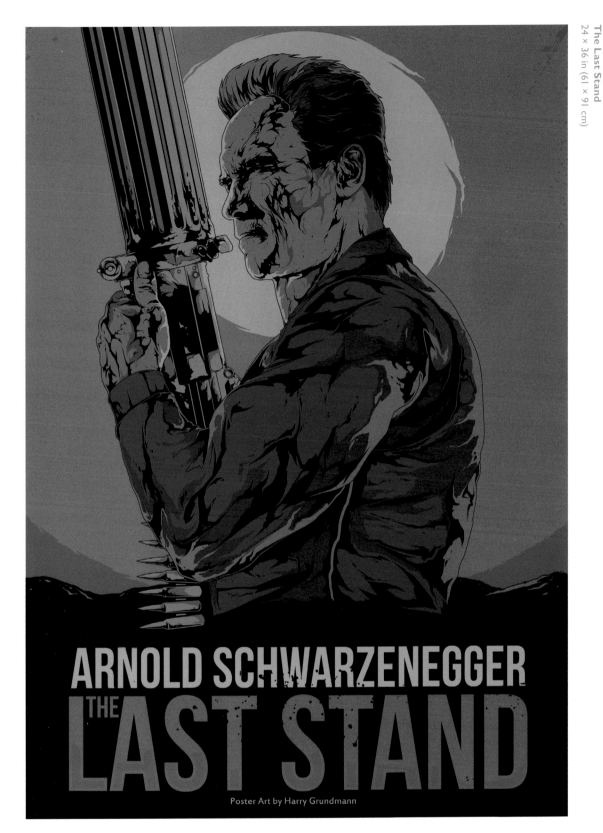

The Last Stand
24 × 36 in (61 × 91 cm)

ARNOLD SCHWARZENEGGER
THE LAST STAND

Poster Art by Harry Grundmann

FIRST FILM: I remember seeing a Russian television miniseries of the Jules Verne novel *In Search of Captain Grant.* Oh, and *Evil Dead 3: Army of Darkness.*

PREFERRED MEDIUM: Adobe Illustrator, Photoshop, Ideas, ink, pencil, and a Wacom Cintiq tablet.

Godzilla
(actual title = *Beast of Burden*)
17 × 23 in (42 × 59 cm)

Andy Hau

DESIGN FIRM	A.H.A. Design Ltd.
LOCATION	London / UK London / UK
SITE	Andyhau.com

コジラ

BEHIND THE POSTERS: *Beast of Burden* was commissioned by *ShortList* magazine for their tribute to *Godzilla*. The modern *Godzilla* films are incredible works of digital wizardry, but as a result they've lost the fun and slightly kitsch aspect of the original movies that made them so endearing. Inspired by this, as well as the architecture of New York, the colors of Toyko, and the vintage Japanese posters for *Godzilla*, I wanted to create a poster that celebrated the exuberance and joy of the original films. *Beast of Burden* comes in two colors: the standard black edition and a gold edition, which is printed on highly reflective mirror board that makes the neon lights in the print sparkle and glitter.

Ceci N'est Past un Poisson was created for Bottleneck Gallery's "It Came From 1984" show. The exhibition happened to fall on the anniversary of my mother's death, and because I have such strong memories of watching *Splash* with her as a child, I knew I had to do something based on this film. A little corny and sentimental, I know, but sometimes artists are! I wanted to create a print that was not obviously aquatic while at the same time celebrated the city of New York, which almost acts as another character in the film. I therefore chose to illustrate only Madison's mermaid form as a blurred reflection in the rain and used bright, clashing neon colors to capture the joy and feel-good atmosphere of the film (and the era).

Splash
(actual title = *Ceci N'est Past un Poisson*)
18 × 24 in (46 × 61 cm)

DESIGN FIRM	A.H.A. Design Ltd.
LOCATION	London / UK London / UK
SITE	Andyhau.com

INFLUENCES: Hayao Miyazaki and Jamie Hewlett provided an endless amount of inspiration for concepts and ideas. I love their grasp of the surreal, which makes their work both achingly beautiful and wonderfully weird. In terms of style, I love Zaha Hadid's early suprematist paintings and their sense of dynamism and weightlessness, not to mention her immaculate control of color.

FAVORITE FILM / GENRE: My favorite film, without a doubt, is *Spirited Away*—it changed my life. I love all animation, but in terms of its storytelling and visual ideas, the movie remains completely unrivalled.

FIRST FILM: It may have been *Lady and the Tramp,* although the main thing I remember is seeing the Siamese cats singing and wondering what on earth was going on. A far more memorable experience was trying to get into *Gremlins 2* with my dad in the early '90s. I was slightly underage at the time, but managed to get in anyway.

PREFERRED MEDIUM: Digital. There is a lot of snobbery regarding hand drawing and screen print—and rightly so —but digital illustration also requires a great amount of skill and technique.

CLIENTS: I have been lucky enough to be commissioned by American Express, Imogen Heap, CoolBrands, *Kiplinger's Personal Finance*, and *Advanced Photoshop* magazine.

ADDITIONAL REMARKS: It is exciting to see artistry come back to movie posters. For the past decade, film posters have been seen as an afterthought, reduced to a twenty-minute collaging exercise in Photoshop spliced with some text. Good movie posters not only celebrate the film they are based on, but also transcend it and become works of art themselves.

Dr. No
41 × 59 in (104 × 150 cm)

ALIAS	Szoki
LOCATION	Budapest / Hungary
SITE	Behance.net/szoki

BEHIND THE POSTERS: I have long been a fan of the *007* movies, and wanted to create a few new posters around the franchise's 50th anniversary.

INFLUENCES: Saul Bass.

Goldfinger
17 × 23 in (43 × 58 cm)

FIRST FILM: My first movie memory is the *The Golden Voyage of Sinbad* that I saw on television, with those great Ray Harryhausen creatures.

PREFERRED MEDIUM: Digital art.

Friday the 13th: The Final Chapter
11 × 17 in (28 × 43 cm)

Nathan Thomas Milliner

| LOCATION | Louisville, Kentucky / US |
| SITE | Rebelrouserart.com |

BEHIND THE POSTERS: In 2014, I was so busy doing commercial work that I hadn't drawn much for myself. Just for fun, I decided to create a 40th anniversary poster of *The Texas Chainsaw Massacre*. Then I decided to do one each month. *Friday the 13th Part IV* [shown here] was an obvious choice, as I have always loved the way Jason looked in that film.

I created the 30th anniversary piece for *A Nightmare on Elm Street* because it is my favorite horror film. I incorporated as many of the murders as I could. So, Tina is being pulled into the bed (similar to Glen's death) by Freddy himself, and Rod is being hanged by the snake-like bed sheets. I also brought in the "extending arms" of Freddy from the film. I had a lot of fun with this piece, and Amanda Wyss (aka Tina) was pleased that a poster finally featured her image. Robert Englund really dug it, too. I was able to get them both a copy when I attended Flashback Weekend in Chicago.

RECENT PROJECTS: People typically know my work from either *HorrorHound* magazine or Scream Factory. I have worked with Scream Factory on eighteen titles to date: *Halloween 2* and *3*, *Terror Train*, *The Funhouse*, *Deadly Blessing*, *The Burning*, *The Howling*, *Day of the Dead*, *Night of the Comet*, *Night of the Demons*, *Sleepaway Camp*, *Dog Soldiers*, *Motel Hell*, *Dolls*, *Shocker*, and *The Garbage Pail Kids Movie*. I have also created several Blu-ray covers internationally in Austria and France. I am currently working on a vinyl album cover, and have created some indie film posters and novel covers as well. I just wrapped up photography on my third film, a short that will be featured in a horror anthology film, *Volumes of Blood*. I co-wrote and directed the segment.

174

A Nightmare on Elm Street
11 × 17 in (28 × 43 cm)

▼

Nathan Thomas Milliner

LOCATION Louisville, Kentucky / US

SITE Rebelrouserart.com

PINCH ME MOMENT: Probably the *Never Sleep Again* book cover; Red Rover Books hired me to do the cover art for their 30th anniversary book about the making of the original film (a dream come true).

I just created some art for Brian O'Halloran, which was cool because I am a major *Clerks* fan. Special effects wizard Greg Nicotero wrote recently to tell me how blown away he was with my website, which he'd spent over an hour browsing through, and inquired about a commission.

Quentin Tarantino is my favorite filmmaker, and recently I was hired by The Weinstein Company to provide art for the Museum of Modern Art's tribute to Tarantino's films in New York. Seeing photos of Quentin, Keitel, Foxx, Buscemi, and the Weinsteins on the red carpet with my artwork behind them was unreal.

CLIENTS: *HorrorHound*, Scream Factory, The Weinstein Company, Fright Rags, NSM Records, Ecstasy of Film, Red Rover Books.

ADDITIONAL REMARKS: I am honored to be part of the second volume of this book. I am shocked that my work in the first book was so well-received, as the talent in volume one was incredible. I want to thank everyone out there for keeping this dead art alive.

BEHIND THE POSTERS: *Nightbreed* was one of the first films I saw in a theater. My mother is a huge horror fan and took me to see it, and to this day it remains a favorite. I once heard the film described as "*Gone with the Wind* with monsters," so *Gone with the Wind*'s film poster was the primary influence for the design. *Nightbreed*'s love story between Boone and Lori was such a prominent factor in Clive Barker's novel, and glimpses of this relationship were seen in the film, so I wanted to make this the main concept. *Nightbreed* is easily one of my favorite movies.

American Psycho. I was in love with *American Psycho*'s story line ever since first seeing the film in 2002. It is also one of the only films that had me running out to purchase the related novel. I couldn't shake my uneasiness with the story. I felt dirty, and I loved it. The poster design here portrays Patrick Bateman's descent into insanity and depravity, made worse by the materialistic world he was desperately trying to be a part of. Bateman's hate and venom is represented as part of his business suit (his status symbol), which slowly morphs him into a wild beast.

LOCATION Universal City, Texas / US

SITE Pittidesart.com

A VINTAGE CONTEMPORARIES ORIGINAL

AMERICAN PSYCHO

A NOVEL BY BRET EASTON ELLIS

TIMOTHY PITTIDES

INFLUENCES: I am influenced by artists such as Brandon Holt, Todd McFarlane, Aaron Horkey, Stephen Platt, Clive Barker, Jim Lee, Jack Kirby, Nicolas Delort, and countless other comic book and film artists.
FAVORITE FILM / GENRE: Horror and science fiction—nothing compares.

FIRST FILM: The first film that I remember seeing on television was *Night of the Living Dead*. *A Nightmare on Elm Street 3: Dream Warriors* was the first in a theater.
PREFERRED MEDIUM: I prefer working in pencil, and then ink. However, I also paint, sculpt, and work in charcoal. Certain ideas and creations fit better with certain mediums.

Labyrinth
18 × 24 in (46 × 61 cm)

DESIGN FIRM Turksworks

LOCATION Carmarthenshire, Wales / UK

SITE Turksworks.co.uk

BEHIND THE POSTERS: These were privately commissioned by an online collector group. They also happen to be films that have meant a great deal to me through the years. I cherished *Labyrinth* in my childhood, while in recent years *Pan's Labyrinth* has become one of my personal favorites. They have a similar theme but are so different in tone. Both are also such visually unique movies that it was a joy to create posters for them. It's as close as you can get to actually working on a movie itself.

INFLUENCES: A lot of my influences come from film: visionary directors such as Guillermo del Toro, David Lynch, and Tim Burton. I also love the beautiful classical poster art of John Alvin, Bob Peak, and of course, Drew Struzan. Growing up during the 1980s and being a *Star Wars* nut, Ralph McQuarrie's work was also a big influence. All wonderful but sadly underrated artists. Aside from movies, I love the work of comic artist Sean Phillips, particularly his stylish take on film noir.

FAVORITE FILM / GENRE: Sci-fi or fantasy. Growing up in the late '70s/'80s, I was a *Star Wars* kid, and those films had a huge effect on me, including all the imitations and rip-offs they spawned. I loved the likes of *Battle Beyond the Stars*, *Battlestar Galactica*, and *The Last Starfighter* This was a great time for sci-fi movies. My favorite all-time film came out of this era, too—*Close Encounters of the Third Kind*. In my eyes, this is as perfect a film as you can get, and I don't think Spielberg has ever done better.

Pan's Labyrinth
18 × 24 in (46 × 61 cm)

FIRST FILM: My first visits to the cinema were almost always Disney-based. The earliest memory that I have is seeing *The Jungle Book*. That beautiful animation, combined with those wonderful songs, created such an impression on me. I wanted to run home and draw after seeing any of those Disney movies. I had sketchbooks full of vibrant Disney characters like Baloo and Mowgli.

PREFERRED MEDIUM: I usually first sketch out ideas in my sketchbook and then work from that point on the computer. I also create textures with inks and paints and then scan them. You can't reproduce those textures on the computer, and quite often I create "happy accidents" that give the final artwork a particular feel. I try to keep these "real" elements a key aspect of my artwork.

CLIENTS: I've been lucky enough to work with some dream clients such as Disney, Legendary Pictures, *Rolling Stone*, and Universal. I have also produced posters for the television channel ITV, as well as magazine covers for the likes of *SciFiNow* and *Retro Gamer*.

ADDITIONAL REMARKS: A part of me feels that I am a frustrated filmmaker, and that creating poster artwork is as close as I can get to directing a movie. You can create a particular tone or feel by using color, brushwork, and textures. There's also a sense of nostalgia to my work, which harks back to the painted movie posters of my childhood. It's all about creating that sense of wonder and excitement again that I regularly experienced as a kid at the movies.

Spaceballs
12 × 18 in (30 × 46 cm)

BEHIND THE POSTERS: For the *Spaceballs* poster, I had a friend that was hosting a public viewing of the movie. I wanted to promote the event in a fun way, so I took on the design challenge of creating the alternative movie print seen here. With *Bride of Frankenstein*, I just love the character that Elsa Lanchester played, and wanted to pay tribute by focusing more on her than the other characters. The print also hints at the sexuality that is carefully avoided in the film.

FAVORITE FILM / GENRE: My favorite films are *Pee-Wee's Big Adventure* and *Dr. Strangelove*, with the *Kill Bill* films following close behind. Right now my favorite genre is low-fi sci-fi, which includes films like *Another Earth*, *Melancholia*, *Upstream Color*, and my favorite, *Primer*.

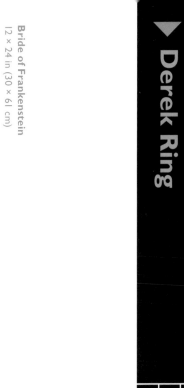

Bride of Frankenstein
12 × 24 in (30 × 61 cm)

FIRST FILM: I watched a lot of Disney movies when I was a kid, and the first was probably *Dumbo*.

PREFERRED MEDIUM: My preferred medium is digital. I work primarily in Adobe Illustrator.
CLIENTS: Lego, Looney Labs.

Derek Eads

World War Z
18 × 24 in (46 × 61 cm)

LOCATION Indiana / US

SITE Derekeads.tumblr.com

BEHIND THE POSTERS: *World War Z.* Zombie films are the best. I didn't understand everyone's predetermined hate for this movie, but I thoroughly enjoyed it.

Kingpin. I love Bill Murray, as anyone who follows my work knows. Every year around Thanksgiving, I have a "Bill Murray Week" on my Tumblr and put together an entire week's worth of Murray art. The man is a legend. I catch something new every time I revisit *Kingpin.* A very underrated comedy.

INFLUENCES: My biggest influence is Margaret Kilgallen. At a time where I was concerned that digital art was the way to go, I stumbled upon the documentary *Beautiful Losers*, and it changed my outlook. She inspired and rekindled my love for hand-drawn lines and lettering. I strongly suggest that anyone interested in art watch this film.

Jordan Crane's work is another influence, with a delightfully funky dream-like feel. He has an honest way of drawing people. I have also been closely following Florey and Paul Ainsworth and am blown away by how much their talent grows from week to week.

Another influence is the filmography of Paul Thomas Anderson, with its beautiful visuals and unique characters. I probably shouldn't have been allowed to watch *Boogie Nights* at such a young age, but I'm glad I was. I have never seen a film crafted so well. Also, Kevin Smith. *Mallrats* was my everything. When I was in high school, I wanted to be Brodie, and I'm not sure if that's changed. Smith's books and podcasts have become a constant source of inspiration/motivation. He's always working. If I catch myself not doing something, his work reminds me to get back to it. And, of course, Wes Anderson. How could anyone watch one of his films and not walk away inspired to create?

182

Kingpin
24 × 18 in (61 × 46 cm)

FAVORITE FILM / GENRE: *Eternal Sunshine of the Spotless Mind.* I could watch this film every day.

FIRST FILM: It's hard to recall a "first film," but I do remember a lot of my youth spent watching and quoting Jim Carrey (*Dumb and Dumber* and *Ace Ventura*).

PREFERRED MEDIUM: Hand drawing. I like to draw everything by hand and then add colors and textures digitally. Style-wise, I try to explore every possible direction. I like the idea of someone seeing my catalog of work and thinking that it was put together by various artists.

CLIENTS: Via Audio. My favorite band, my first client, and largely responsible for my career in art. I had an immediate connection to their lyrics and have drawn an insane amount of inspiration from them. Thank you, Jessica Martins.

Lucius. You will never meet more wonderfully kind or talented people. Their amount of talent will throw you into a jealous rage.

The Spring Standards. I love this band. If not just for their heartwarming music, then for the amount of nurturing trust they have in my art. I've been able to work on an abundance of projects with them and always look forward to the next.

Thanks to these three bands I have been able to work with several additional musicians, like Jukebox the Ghost, Elizabeth & the Catapult, Inland Traveler, Michaela Anne, Annie Lynch, and Dear Georgiana, among others. I also regularly contribute original artwork and screen prints to shows at Gallery 1988, Bottleneck, Hero Complex, and Ltd. Art Gallery.

BRAND	Grey Cardigan
LOCATION	Cleveland, Ohio / US
SITE	Greycardigan.com

OLIVIA **NEWTON–JOHN** ✹ JOHN **TRAVOLTA**

grease

RECORDED IN RYDELL HIGH-FI STEREO

directed by **RANDAL KLEISER** *musical by* **JIM JACOBS + WARREN CASEY**

RH

BEHIND THE POSTERS: *Grease* holds a very special place in my heart. I fondly recall getting into my pajamas when it was still light outside, boarding my family's silver Cutlass in the summer of 1978, and seeing the just released *Grease* at the drive-in! I was only three years old, but I recall it so vividly—in particular the "Hopelessly Devoted To You" scene. Olivia Newton-John's white nightgown against the nighttime backdrop was so stark and striking to me. Even then I appreciated a good cinematic palette and a flair for the dramatic, I suppose! I used to live for that annual broadcast of *Grease* on network television. In a pre-cable/DVD/Internet world – the airing of iconic movies was such an epic event. I almost find it a bit unfortunate that said magic has been lost in this era of instant accessibility.

Grease 2 tends to have the reputation of the ugly duckling younger sibling to the original, but I love it for what it is and hold the same sentimentality for it that I do for the original. In my *Grease* posters, I liked the idea of depicting the high school social status of the main characters through their apparel.

INFLUENCES: I draw much of my inspiration from mid-twentieth-century aesthetics. Clothing, color palettes, patterns, and simplicity of form prevalent in that era act as my muse. The minimalism of Swiss design aesthetic is certainly influential on my work. I appreciate the personal signature that directors such as Tim Burton and Baz Luhrmann curate into their films. Fashion designer Thom Browne's employment of classic styling infused with the avant garde always leaves me in love.

MICHELLE **PFEIFFER** ✲ MAXWELL **CAULFIELD**

*grease*²

RECORDED IN RYDELL HIGH-FI STEREO

directed by **PATRICIA BIRCH**   *original screenplay by* **KEN FINKLEMAN**

RH

Grease 2
18 × 20 in (46 × 51 cm)

▼

Brian Andrew Jasinski

BRAND Grey Cardigan
LOCATION Cleveland, Ohio / US
SITE Greycardigan.com

FAVORITE FILM / GENRE: Not surprisingly, films from the 1950–60s are amongst my favorite, such as the styling and aesthetics of films by Alfred Hitchcock, Elia Kazan, and Douglas Sirk. There was such a precise attention to detail and staging during this period, and this has influenced my work. Flashing forward, the body of work by John Hughes would also fall into the category of films that, like *Grease*, hold a place of fond nostalgia with me.

PREFERRED MEDIUM: Many of my illustrations are digitally created – I also enjoy working in graphite, watercolor, and gouache. I love seeing how my style evolves and translates in different "languages" depending on the medium.

ADDITIONAL REMARKS: The idea of artists reinventing movie posters is fantastic! Over the years, the artistry of the movie poster has fallen victim to "star power"—and posters tend to be a simple collage of the actors in a film. Posters used to have much more of a clever nature about them. I love seeing how an artist's eye reinterprets a film, and enjoy picking up on the details and nods to a film that they place into their pieces!

Scott Woolston

An American Werewolf in London
27 × 40 in (69 × 102 cm)

LOCATION | West Yorkshire / UK

SITE | Scottwoolston.proSite.com

BEHIND THE POSTERS: Both of these films haunted and mystified me. I watched *An American Werewolf in London* when I was younger and was strongly affected by its eerie strangeness. I had never seen anything quite like it. Many years later, *Valhalla Rising* had the same effect. Mads Mikkelsen's stare plus the film's use of color (especially red) captivated me. Oh yeah, and they both had some good gory moments.

INFLUENCES: I have always been influenced by graphic design, film, and music. Here is a short list of influences that quickly come to mind: Steven Spielberg, Stanley Kubrick, Quentin Tarantino, Ennio Morricone, Saul Bass, David Carson, Otl Aicher, Bruce Lee, New York City, graffiti, '80s and '90s hip-hop music, and Japanese Chirashi/mini posters.

FAVORITE FILM / GENRE: I wrestle with a top five or top ten all the time. The only film that I don't have to question is my number one: *Jaws*.

FIRST FILM: I honestly think it could be *The Wizard of Oz*, but it could also be *Indiana Jones and the Temple of Doom*, *The Neverending Story*, *Star Wars*, or *E.T.* I know that I also wore out my VHS copy of *The Last Starfighter*.

186

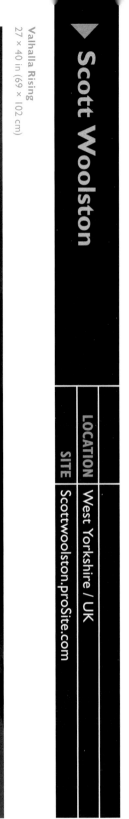

Valhalla Rising
27 × 40 in (69 × 102 cm)

Scott Woolston

LOCATION West Yorkshire / UK

SITE Scottwoolston.proSite.com

PREFERRED MEDIUM: Adobe Photoshop / Illustrator.

CLIENTS: For my day job I work as a film poster designer. A lot of people berate modern poster design and I would agree that much of what is produced is truly forgettable. But, oh man, you should see the cutting room floor! There are so many talented designers, behind the scenes, creating incredible stuff.

Through the day job I have worked with various London-based agencies and with directors and producers working on smaller budget projects. I design alternative posters in my own time. Mostly for fun, but sometimes out of pure frustration with the industry.

ADDITIONAL REMARKS: I love the fact that alternative film posters have made the industry stand up and take notice. Who needs to own the official poster anymore? Just create your own.

Gladiator
13 × 20 in (33 × 51 cm)

BEHIND THE POSTERS: The *Gladiator* poster was originally from a school project in my portfolio class. We were assigned a year in which we had to illustrate a movie poster for the Academy Award winner for Best Picture. In my case the year was 2000. With *Gladiator*, I really enjoyed the visuals of the scenes taking place in Germany, and wanted my image to be different from existing *Gladiator* posters (which tend to focus on the Colosseum). I thought that having Maximus performing his war ritual [i.e., rubbing his hands with dirt] on the poster would give viewers a taste of his character and hopefully create a more intimate connection.

The *Alien* poster was created specifically for this book. At first I picked *Alien* simply because I like the film. I soon realized that *Alien* was not just another Ridley Scott movie, but a career-defining picture for him.

I thought that it was important to portray the alien as a clever predator, but at the time not reveal the alien in full. I chose to create a close-up of the alien capturing Ripley by using its tail, thus hinting at the ominous creature without spoiling the full creature design.

INFLUENCES: Many artists that have influenced me, such as Rembrandt, Donato Giancola, Justin Gerard, Morris, Hergé, and Frank Miller. Writer/illustrator Don Rosa, with his unique Disney comics, captivated me and led me to realize that I wanted to be an artist. Artists like Pink Floyd, Genesis, and Nick Cave have inspired me with their music, while Christopher Nolan, Ridley Scott, and the Coen brothers have done the same with their films.

Thomas Kirkeberg

LOCATION Tønsberg / Norway

SITE Thomaskirkeberg.com

FAVORITE FILM / GENRE: When pressed into a corner, it would have to be sci-fi, as well as fantasy. I love being taken into new and amazing worlds. *The Lord of the Rings*, both the movies and the books, are probably my favorites, though I also absolutely love *O' Brother, Where Art Thou?* and the Australian western *The Proposition*.

FIRST FILM: Most likely *Pinchcliffe Grand Prix*, a Norwegian stop motion film from 1975. The story involves bicycle repairman and inventor Theodore Rimspoke who, with his friends, create a race car to challenge a rival in a grand prix. It's a lovely movie, full of amazing detail, humor, and music. I was crazy about it as a child and have seen it endless times (along with *Asterix vs. Caesar*, which was on the same tape).

PREFERRED MEDIUM: I am most comfortable with digital, but I also enjoy ink and watercolor. Lately I have been experimenting with acrylic and oil paint.

CLIENTS: My most notable client is Cappelen Damm, a major publishing house in Norway.

189

The Cabin in the Woods
24 × 36 in (61 × 91 cm)

DESIGN FIRM Hopko Designs

LOCATION Cortland, New York / US

SITE Hopkodesigns.com

INFLUENCES: Drew Struzan, Bob Peak, Richard Amsel, Dan Gouzee, Ridley Scott, Martin Scorsese, Albert Brooks, Brian De Palma, George Lucas, Alfred Hitchcock, Woody Allen, and Steven Spielberg.

FAVORITE FILM / GENRE: Films I love: *Jaws, The Empire Strikes Back, Goodfellas, Raiders of the Lost Ark, Back to the Future, Alien, North by Northwest, 2001: A Space Odyssey, The Thing, Night of the Creeps, Glengarry Glen Ross,* and *Crimes and Misdemeanors.*

FIRST FILM: The film that made me love movies is *Star Wars.* My uncle was a projectionist and took my cousin and I to work with him one Saturday back in the summer of 1977 and we watched *Star Wars* all day—the matinee, 7:00 p.m., and 9:00 p.m. shows—three times in one day! I was seven years old and totally inspired.

Swingers
24 × 36 in (61 × 91 cm)

DESIGN FIRM Hopko Designs
LOCATION Cortland, New York / US
SITE Hopkodesigns.com

PREFERRED MEDIUM: I love oil paint, but these day I work on the Wacom tablet.

CLIENTS: For the past sixteen years I have run Hopko Designs, an advertising and design studio. Clients are mostly from the Central New York area.

ADDITIONAL REMARKS: Proud to be a member of the now-famous Poster Posse.

Cowboy Bebop
(actual title = *Whatever Happens, Happens*)
18 × 24 in (46 × 61 cm)

▼ **Joshua Budich**

LOCATION Woodstock, Maryland / US

SITE Joshuabudich.com

BEHIND THE POSTERS: *To See with Eyes Unclouded by Hate* [*Princess Mononoke*] and *Whatever Happens, Happens* [*Cowboy Bebop*] are my favorite pieces from my 2014 solo show "Otaku Obscura" with Spoke Art. With the *Mononoke* piece, I wanted to challenge myself by changing up my process, specifically with no key line, but also by utilizing a painterly, almost watercolor approach to the colors and shading. The *Cowboy Bebop* piece could be considered a more "traditional" style of screen print design, but I pushed myself, and my printer, with the modified halftone/overprinting techniques that we have been developing together over the past few years.

Finally, *They're Here to Save the World* (*Ghostbusters*) [see page 2] was an incredible collaboration with Gallery 1988 for their *Ghostbusters* 30th anniversary show. This piece was an ambitious attempt to get all of the actors to sign off on their likenesses, which fortunately we accomplished only days before the untimely passing of Harold Ramis. I am extremely proud to have been part of this project.

RECENT PROJECTS: This year I've had some big opportunities to work with the usual suspects, as well as with some new clients. Gallery 1988's *Ghostbusters* 30th anniversary show was a fantastic chance to flex my portraiture muscles. Another great opportunity was working with Skuzzles for the first time on a redesign of horror film classics—MGM/Fox's Halloween series of Blu-ray covers. Also, I finished up my *Star Wars*

Joshua Budich

LOCATION Woodstock, Maryland / US

SITE Joshuabudich.com

▲ **Princess Mononoke**
(actual title = *To See with Eyes Unclouded by Hate*)
18 × 24 in (46 × 61 cm)

もののけ姫

OTC triptych with Art v Cancer, created a commissioned *Indiana Jones* triptych series, and received a serendipitous Twitter invitation from one Zach Braff to collaborate with him on a screen print for his latest film, *Wish I Was Here.*

PINCH ME MOMENT: Since I live on the East Coast and most of my fan base (as well as the galleries I primarily work with) are on the West Coast, I do not get many opportunities to meet fans in person. However, traveling to San Francisco for the opening of my "Otaku Obscura" show at Spoke Art was an incredible experience. Another event of note was being interviewed for *Twenty-Four by Thirty-Six*, an upcoming documentary on the art and artists of the screen print world.

IS THE FILM INDUSTRY COMING ALONG? After having a great conversation with Zach Braff about how we lament the fact that movie posters have become so much of an afterthought with the film studios these days, I believe there's about to be a big, fantastic shift in how the film industry views working with traditional artists on the artwork/posters for their projects.

CLIENTS: Spoke Art Gallery, Gallery 1988, The Oscars, Adidas, Universal Studios, Zach Braff.

DESIGN FIRM	Ink Rituals & Viral Graphics
LOCATION	Athens / Greece & San Francisco, California / US
SITE	Inkrituals.com

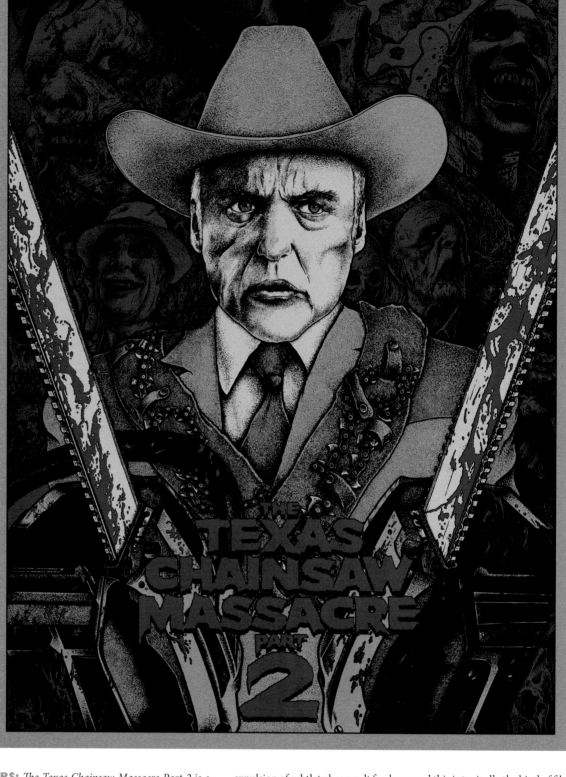

BEHIND THE POSTERS: *The Texas Chainsaw Massacre Part 2* is a sequel scorned by many. Leatherface has evolved from a brute, creepy force of Texan destruction [in Part I] to a perverted, sexually befuddled, crazed dancer. The washed out and subdued grainy visual charm of the original has been replaced by technicolor and over-the-top bone backdrops. All of the horror that the original let us create in our minds through insinuation is now washed out in a cacophony of blood and gore. The hitchhiker, a disturbing nightmare too close to reality, is replaced by his brother, Chop Top, an altogether more colorful nightmare in a Sonny Bono wig. And then, there's ex-Texas Ranger Lieutenant Lefty Enright. A triple-chainsaw-wielding Dennis Hopper, completely out of his mind, chewing up scenery both literally and metaphorically. To most, all of this might sound terrible. But this total

expulsion of subtlety has a cult fan base, and this is typically the kind of film I enjoy tackling. The poster needed to be as "in your face" as the film, and I went for visual overload. I wanted the layout, detail, and color to work toward portraying the two antagonists' confrontation. Everything was hand-drawn with 0.005 to 0.08 Microns on Bristol board, at the actual print size of 18 × 24 inches, then was colored digitally for screen printing.

Alan Parker's 1987 horror-noir *Angel Heart* has always been at the top of the list of films I need to make posters for. As an underrated movie, barely any alternative posters have been made for it. This is odd, as the movie boasts powerful visuals, a vast thematic depth, and an interesting overall aesthetic. It's essentially what I like to call "identity horror," wherein the true horror takes place in the protagonist's mind as he slowly discovers himself. All this is wrapped in a sweaty, bloody, and dirty film noir puzzle that we slowly piece together along with Harry Angel. The main burning heart illustration is made

DESIGN FIRM	Ink Rituals & Viral Graphics
LOCATION	Athens / Greece & San Francisco, California / US
SITE	Inkrituals.com

of objects that play a prominent role in how Harry Angel delves deeper into his mystery. The dog tag, the voodoo candles, the egg, the feathers, the eyes, the straight-razor, the elevator—all unlock the full picture. Similar to *The Texas Chainsaw Massacre Part 2*, everything in *Angel Heart* was hand-drawn with 0.005 to 0.08 Microns on Bristol board, at the actual print size of 18 × 24 inches, and then colored digitally.

INFLUENCES: Here's a select few that come to mind (I felt I needed to add some musicians to the mix as they influence me *while* I work): Austin Osman Spare, Bernie Wrightson, Darkthrone, John Carpenter, Jack Kirby, Melvins, Stanley Kubrick, Brainbombs, John Buscema, Swans, Lucio Fulci, Shinya Tsukamoto, Glenn Fabry, Death, Amando De Ossorio, Ian Miller, Celtic Frost, David Cronenberg, Nick Blinko, Takashi Miike, Aaron Horkey, Kiyoshi Kurosawa.

FAVORITE FILM / GENRE: Horror is my most and least favorite genre. My favorite film alternates between *The Thing* and the original *Dawn of the Dead*.
FIRST FILM: Non-revamped *Star Wars* on VHS.
PREFERRED MEDIUM: Hands, pencils, ink, and paper.
CLIENTS: Melvins, Swans, Soundgarden, Coffins, Grief, Mudhoney, and more (mostly band-related artwork).

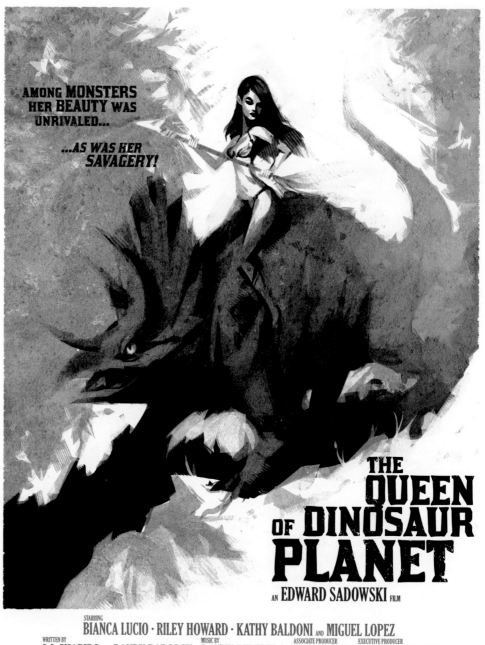

AMONG MONSTERS
HER BEAUTY WAS
UNRIVALED...

...AS WAS HER
SAVAGERY!

THE
QUEEN
OF DINOSAUR
PLANET

AN EDWARD SADOWSKI FILM

STARRING
BIANCA LUCIO · RILEY HOWARD · KATHY BALDONI AND MIGUEL LOPEZ
WRITTEN BY
J.J. SHAPIRO AND RANDY BABCOCK
MUSIC BY
DANNY BELZBERG
ASSOCIATE PRODUCER
NINA WICHT
EXECUTIVE PRODUCER
MICKEY LE ROUX
PRODUCED BY
JAMES DE LA ROSA
DIRECTED BY
EDWARD SADOWSKI
A VON DART RELEASE
© 1977 VON DART PICTURES
R RESTRICTED
UNDER 17 REQUIRES ACCOMPANYING
PARENT OR ADULT GUARDIAN

BEHIND THE POSTERS: I really just wanted to draw some pretty girls and monsters, so the origin of the ideas weren't too interesting. However for the *Giant Mutants* poster [right] I asked my girlfriend (now wife) to pose as reference for the girl character, but I needed to find a helmet for her to wear. I went on Craigslist and found a cool Vespa helmet nearby, and when I went to pick it up, it turned out that the guy selling it was James Raymond, son of David Crosby. I got to see his studio and we talked a bit about how he toured with his dad. He also was excited to see the final illustration!

INFLUENCES: Bob Peak, Bernie Fuchs, Robert McGinnis, Frank Frazetta, *Ultraman*, *Gamera*, *Jurassic Park*.
FAVORITE FILM / GENRE: I have a special place in my heart for *E.T.* I love that dude.
FIRST FILM: *Star Wars*.

196

Giant Mutants from Beneath the Earth
19 × 13 (48 × 33 cm)

PREFERRED MEDIUM: I do all of my work in Photoshop.
CLIENTS: Dreamworks, Cartoon Network, Pixar, Laika, FOX, Spike Jonze, Disney.

ADDITIONAL REMARKS: I did these posters at a time in my life when I was still trying to find myself and was exploring a lot of different styles, techniques, and ideas. There are lots of things I'm not proud of, but I'm glad that at least these posters are fun and don't take themselves too seriously. Also, I think I did an okay job drawing that triceratops.

Hostel
27 × 39 in (65 × 98 cm)
A FrightFest Originals release

LOCATION Brighton, East Sussex / UK

SITE Lukeinsect.com + Lukeinsect.bigcartel.com

BEHIND THE POSTERS: Both commissions were for FrightFest Originals. I had previously designed sleeve art for Death Waltz Recordings' vinyl reissue of the sound track *The Living Dead at Manchester Morgue*, and Alex [from FrightFest] asked if I wanted to tackle a reinvention of a cult horror film poster. I was surprised when he mentioned that it was the cult Aussie killer pig horror flick, *Razorback* [right]! I hadn't heard mention of *Razorback* for ages, but it was a favorite of mine back in the '80s when I stayed up late to watch it on television. It's a great movie, beautifully

shot, and directed by Russell Mulcahy, who went on to direct cult fave *Highlander*. I wanted to create something fully illustrated and organic, and went from paper to woodcut without relying on my computer for once.

With *Hostel*, I got another call from Alex. Director Eli Roth was coming for a FrightFest screening of his cannibal horror film *The Green Inferno*, so we thought we'd tackle a reinvention of *Hostel*, the nasty that put him on the map. I looked to Eastern European movie poster art for inspiration, to tie in the movie location.

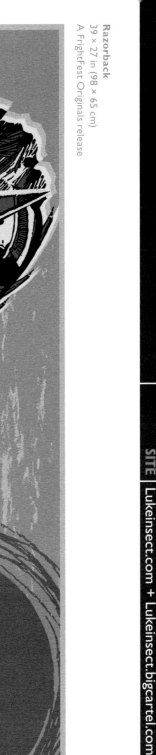

LOCATION Brighton, East Sussex / UK

SITE Lukeinsect.com + Lukeinsect.bigcartel.com

Razorback
39 × 27 in (98 × 65 cm)
A FrightFest Originals release

UAA FILM LIMITED PRESENTS A MCELROY PRODUCTION / RAZORBACK
GREGORY HARRISON / ARKIE WHITELEY / ALSO STARRING BILL KERR / CHRIS HAYWOOD / DAVID ARGUE / JUDY MORRIS AS BETH / SCREENPLAY BY EVERETT DE ROCHE FROM A NOVEL BY PETER BRENNAN
CINEMATOGRAPHY BY DEAN SEMLER / MUSIC BY IVA DAVIES / ASSOCIATE PRODUCER TIM SANDERS / PRODUCED BY HAL MCELROY / DIRECTED BY RUSSELL MULCAHY

INFLUENCES: Sergio Toppi, Hannah Hoch, Dario Argento, Lucio Fulci, Jan Lenica, Roman Polanski, Hans Arp.
FAVORITE FILM / GENRE: Horror!
FIRST FILM: *The Humanoid* starring Richard Kiel, at the ABC Wimbledon cinema.
PREFERRED MEDIUM: Analogue in style, digital in method. But screen print rules all.

CLIENTS: I work mainly for the music industry designing sleeve art for bands. Some recent campaigns include The Prodigy, Enter Shikari, Carl Barat, and James. My first foray into film came when Kenn Goodall and I (collaborating under the name Twins of Evil) were asked to design the poster art for Ben Wheatley's *A Field in England* after he'd seen our reinvention of the poster for *Witchfinder General*. We've since collaborated with him on sleeve art for soundtrack releases to his films *Kill List* and *Sightseers*.

BEHIND THE POSTERS: I wanted to replicate the look and feel of old, beaten up, messy posters that have been on the grindhouse circuit for years. I thought these two films would fit perfectly with that concept, since they're both a bit rough around the edges (in the best way possible).

INFLUENCES: Graham Humphreys. You can always tell when a poster was created by Graham Humphreys. He has such a incredible, unique art style. If I had half the talent that he does, I would be very happy.

LOCATION Nottingham / UK
SITE Bewarethehorrorblog.tumblr.com

FAVORITE FILM / GENRE: It's easy to see from my posters that I am a huge horror fan. I love '80s horror. This includes *The Return of the Living Dead*, *Re-Animator*, *Evil Dead II*, *The Fly*, *Friday the 13th Part 4*, *The Burning*, *An American Werewolf in London*, *Creepshow*, *The Lost Boys*, *The Thing*, *Hellraiser*, and *Fright Night*. However, my favorite film of all time is *The Texas Chainsaw Massacre* (1974), for its simplicity. There are no tricks or gimmicks, just pure terror.

FIRST FILM: My first horror movie was *A Nightmare on Elm Street*. I also have strong memories of watching Michael Jackson's *Thriller* at a very young age. It scared the hell out of me.
PREFERRED MEDIUM: Mostly digital with the occasional pencil drawing. I like to keep it simple.

Tony Agüero

ALIAS TOMO77

LOCATION Costa Rica & Portland, Oregon / US

SITE Tomo77.com

Walk the Line
24 × 36 in (61 × 91 cm)

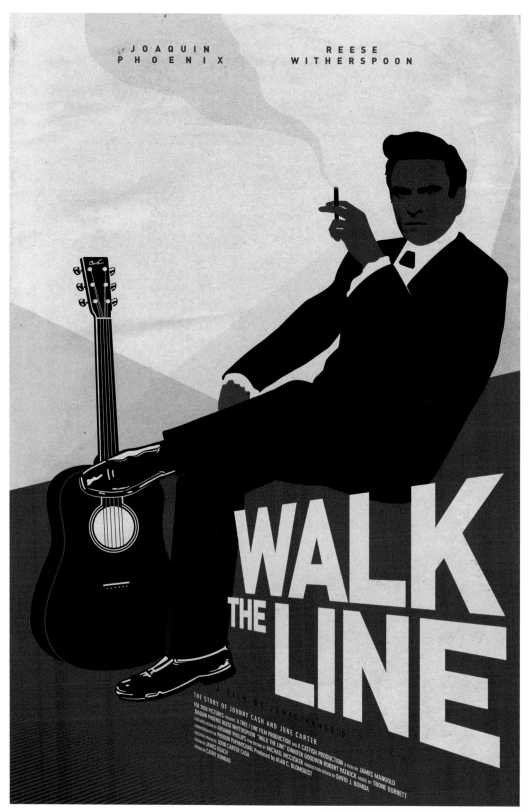

BEHIND THE POSTERS: There is lot of great artwork around current feature films and cult movies, but it's rare to see alternative posters for music-related movies. I was inspired to approach this genre of film, thinking that both *Walk the Line* and *Control* deserved alternative versions. Also, these two pieces were specifically created for this book.

INFLUENCES: Kubrick, music in general, colors, The Designers Republic, cyberpunk, Sixpack France, and Mamoru Oshii. Numerous designers also influence my work. However, I always think that famous designers are colleagues, not rock stars.

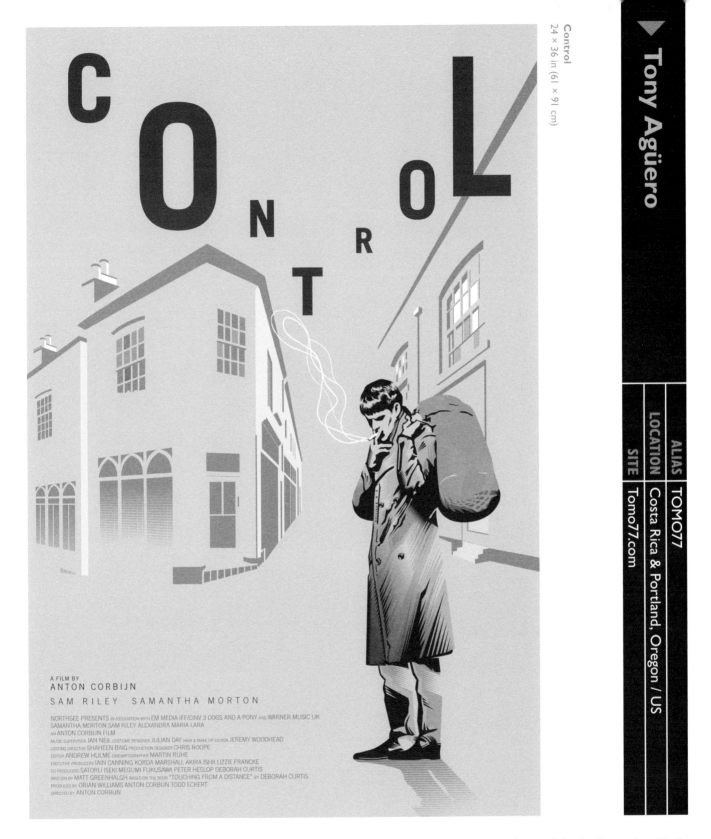

Control
24 × 36 in (61 × 91 cm)

Tony Agüero

ALIAS	TOMO77
LOCATION	Costa Rica & Portland, Oregon / US
SITE	Tomo77.com

A FILM BY
ANTON CORBIJN

SAM RILEY   SAMANTHA MORTON

NORTHSEE PRESENTS IN ASSOCIATION WITH EM MEDIA IFF/CINV 3 DOGS AND A PONY AND WARNER MUSIC UK
SAMANTHA MORTON SAM RILEY ALEXANDRA MARIA LARA
AN ANTON CORBIJN FILM
MUSIC SUPERVISOR IAN NEIL COSTUME DESIGNER JULIAN DAY HAIR & MAKE UP DESIGN JEREMY WOODHEAD
CASTING DIRECTOR SHAHEEN BAIG PRODUCTION DESIGNER CHRIS ROOPE
EDITOR ANDREW HULME CINEMATOGRAPHER MARTIN RUHE
EXECUTIVE PRODUCERS IAIN CANNING KORDA MARSHALL AKIRA ISHII LIZZIE FRANCKE
CO PRODUCERS SATORU ISEKI MEGUMI FUKUSAWA PETER HESLOP DEBORAH CURTIS
WRITTEN BY MATT GREENHALGH BASED ON THE BOOK "TOUCHING FROM A DISTANCE" BY DEBORAH CURTIS
PRODUCED BY ORIAN WILLIAMS ANTON CORBIJN TODD ECKERT
DIRECTED BY ANTON CORBIJN

FAVORITE FILM / GENRE: *The Matrix, Ghost in the Shell, Nosferatu,* and all that is cyberpunk.
FIRST FILM: *Pink Floyd–The Wall.*
PREFERRED MEDIUM: I like to work with mixed media. First I illustrate, followed by some iPad doodling, and then I finish digitally.

ADDITIONAL REMARKS: I design all day (both at work and in the evening). Design is hard work, but I also consider it a lifestyle. Creating alternative movie posters is quite a challenge, and communicating an accurate message should be the goal. However, I prefer more abstract and complex ideas rather than blasting a full image of an actor onto the page.

AllCity

The Neon Demon
An AllCity release
24 × 36 in (61 × 91 cm)

LOCATION London / UK

SITE Allcitymedia.com

THE WICKED DIE YOUNG

THE NEON DEMON
NICOLAS WINDING REFN

BEHIND THE POSTERS: French film distributor Gaumont commissioned us to create a poster for Nicolas Winding Refn's *The Neon Demon*. Although the movie was still in pre-production stage, Refn wanted an image to help launch the project at industry film markets. Stemming from the relationship built through our collaboration on *Only God Forgives* [see page 111], we worked with Refn to create a poster that encapsulates the plastic fantasy and dangerous obsession with beauty that exists in Los Angeles' dark underbelly.

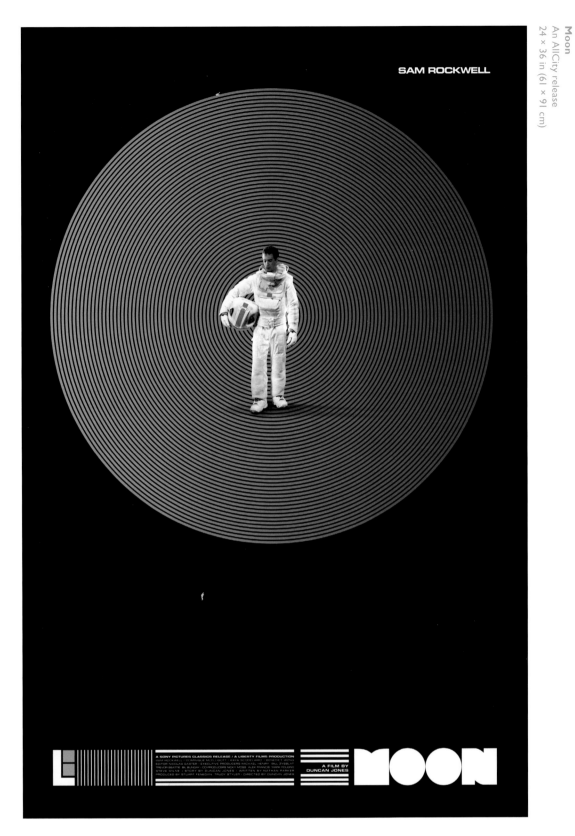

Moon
An AllCity release
24 × 36 in (61 × 91 cm)

SAM ROCKWELL

A SONY PICTURES CLASSICS RELEASE / A LIBERTY FILMS PRODUCTION
SAM ROCKWELL · DOMINIQUE MCELLIGOTT · KAYA SCODELARIO · BENEDICT WONG
EDITOR NICOLAS GASTER · EXECUTIVE PRODUCERS MICHAEL HENRY · BILL ZYSBLAT
TREVOR BEATTIE · BIL BUNGAY · CO-PRODUCERS NICKY MOSS · ALEX FRANCIS · MARK YOUNG
STEVE MILNE · STORY BY DUNCAN JONES · WRITTEN BY NATHAN PARKER
PRODUCED BY STUART FENEGAN · TRUDY STYLER · DIRECTED BY DUNCAN JONES

A FILM BY
DUNCAN JONES

MOON

When we created the film market creative for *Moon*, we also had unseen alternative concepts. Sony chose one of those concepts, "The Rings" [shown here], for their release art, which they adapted to suit. We later partnered with Mondo to produce a redrawn version. Martin Ansin was commissioned to translate the image to a screen print, with gold rings and a glow-in-the-dark variant (printed by D & L). *Empire* magazine recently voted it number three in the best posters of the last twenty-five years.

LOCATION Columbus, Ohio / US

SITE Brianewing.com

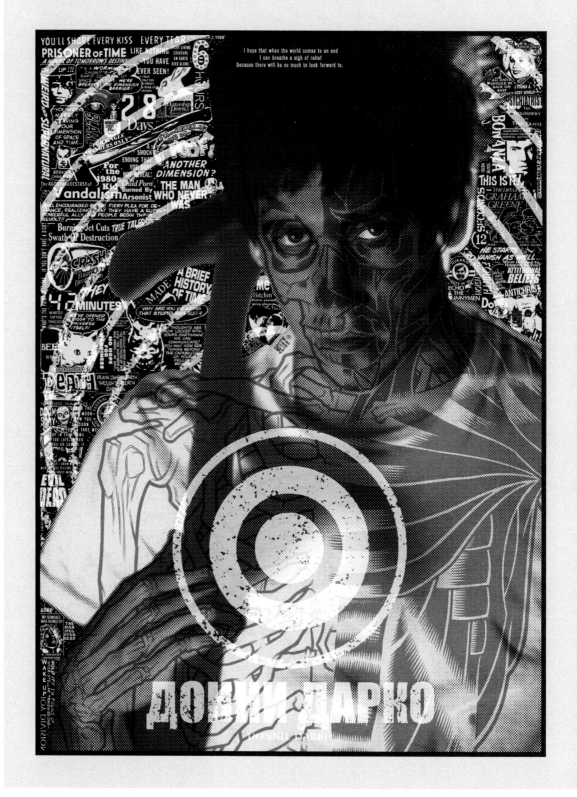

BEHIND THE POSTERS: For *Donnie Darko*, I was putting together ideas for a solo show and had always wanted to make a Darko poster. So, I checked to see what other prints had already been created and felt that the movie hadn't been done justice (yet). If you look closely at the background collage you will see a lot of direct references to the movie, as well as to time travel.

With *Taxi Driver*, I was asked to participate in a group show for Martin Scorsese curated by Spoke Art Gallery. At the time I was just beginning to develop the anatomical style shown here. After reading numerous interviews with the *Taxi Driver* filmmakers, I decided to focus on screenwriter Paul Schrader's description that the character of Travis Bickle was an extension of the alienation and loneliness that he felt in his twenties. This was something I could relate to (sans the killing spree). When news of the show posted online, a friend who worked at the Tribeca Film Festival with De Niro asked that I send him a copy of the *Taxi Driver* print. A few days later I received an email saying that De Niro had framed the print and hung it in his office. That made my year.

INFLUENCES: I could fill this book with all of the influences that I enjoy. For the pieces here I would choose (for obvious reasons) Martin Scorsese and Richard Kelly. Also, a healthy dose of Warhol, Print Mafia, Morning Breath, and FAILE.

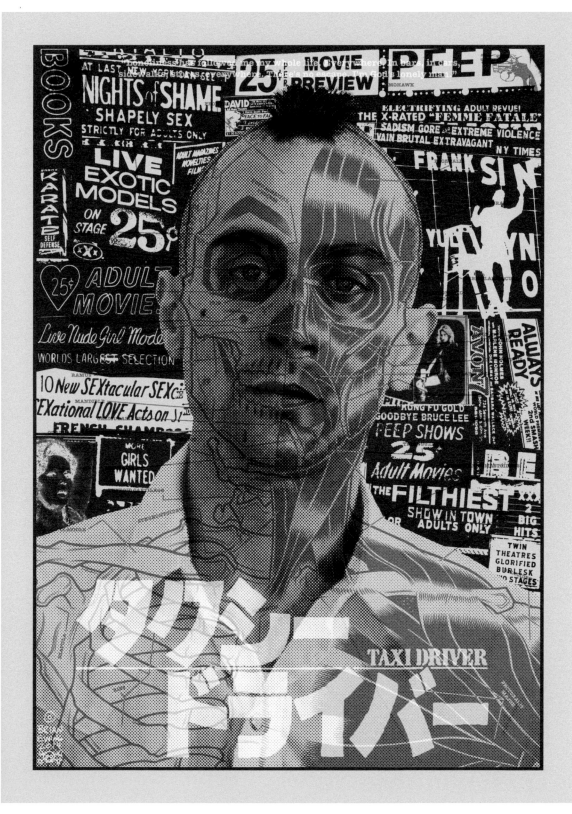

Taxi Driver
18 × 24 in (46 × 61 cm)

FAVORITE FILM / GENRE: Film noir, anime, and Universal Monster movies.
FIRST FILM: The first film I saw in a theater was *American Graffiti*. After that: *Flash Gordon* and *Grease*.
PREFERRED MEDIUM: Whatever I can get my hands on. I make rock posters for a living and art prints for gallery shows. I also own a toy company.

CLIENTS: Warped Tour, Hustler, Playboy, Dark Horse, AT&T, Channel 4, Taste of Chaos, Sprint, Samsung, Vans, Cingular, KIA Motors, DC Comics, Barely Legal, Marvel Comics, Harper Collins, The New Yorker, EMI, BYO, Suicide Girls, DC Shoes, Square Enix, Evil Ink, Vannen Watches, and a million bands.
ADDITIONAL REMARKS: When I saw the first volume of *Alternative Movie Posters*, I was (professionally) jealous to see all of the great artwork collected for the book. I wanted to be in that company. I am grateful to be in the pages of this second volume.

INDEX & CREDITS

Other Schiffer Books by the Author:
Alternative Movie Posters: Film Art from the Underground,
    978-0-7643-4566-1
*Put the Needle on the Record: The 1980s at 45 Revolutions
    Per Minute,* 978-0-7643-3831-1

Other Schiffer Books on Related Subjects:
VHS: Video Cover Art, 1980s to Early 1990s, Thomas "The
    Dude Designs" Hodge, 978-0-7643-4867-9
The World's Rarest Movie Posters, Todd Spoor,
    978-0-7643-3498-6
Hollywood Movie Posters: 1914–1990, Miles Barton,
    978-0-7643-2010-1

Copyright © 2015 by Matthew Chojnacki

Library of Congress Control Number: 2013944509

Cover: Movie poster by Steve Dressler
On the Back Cover:
Top row (left to right): *Dr. Strangelove* / Tracie Ching, *Dawn of the Planet Apes* /
Orlando Arocena, *Groundhog Day* / Andrew Fairclough
Bottom row (left to right): *The Goonies* / Studiohouse Designs, *The Exorcist* / NE,
It / Keith Ten Eyck

Designed by Justin Watkinson
Type set in Gill Sans Std/Minion Pro

ISBN: 978-0-7643-4986-7
Printed in China

Published by Schiffer Publishing, Ltd.
4880 Lower Valley Road
Atglen, PA 19310
Phone: (610) 593-1777; Fax: (610) 593-2002
E-mail: Info@schifferbooks.com

For our complete selection of fine books on this and related subjects, please visit our
webSite at www.schifferbooks.com. You may also write for a free catalog.

This book may be purchased from the publisher. Please try your bookstore first.

We are always looking for people to write books on new and related subjects. If you
have an idea for a book, please contact us at proposals@schifferbooks.com.

Schiffer Publishing's titles are available at special discounts for bulk purchases for
sales promotions or premiums. Special editions, including personalized covers,
corporate imprints, and excerpts can be created in large quantities for special needs.
For more information, contact the publisher.